THE GODFATHER'S WISDOM

MARK SOMERVILLE

The Godfather's Wisdom

Copyright © 2025 Mark Somerville

Editing and Design by Jansina of Rivershore Books

Library of Congress Control Number: 2025925012

ISBN: 978-1-63522-098-8

Printed in the United States of America
10   9   8   7   6   5   4   3   2   1

RIVERSHORE BOOKS

Rivershore Books
8982 Van Buren St. NE • Minneapolis, MN 55434
612-208-3434 • info@rivershorebooks.com

DEDICATION

For my beautiful godchildren George, Ally, and Lily. For my beloved wife Jenny. For all godparents and godchildren. For Saint Carlo Acutis. Proverbs 4:7. To my fellow Eagle Scout, Charlie Kirk: May your legacy serve as an inspiration for generations to engage in civil discourse.

FOREWORD

My beloved godchildren, whom I love deeply,

As you continue to grow into the remarkable individuals that God has designed you to be, I wish to impart a precious gift: the gift of wisdom. This is not just any wisdom, but one that will draw you nearer to God. I share this with you as someone who has gathered these insights over more than fifty years. These lessons are timeless, applicable at any stage of life and in any circumstance. They will guide you on your journey, acting as a compass during both joyous and challenging moments.

It is my hope that these teachings reach anyone seeking a closer relationship with God. Just as one would not cover a lit candle with a bucket, I encourage you to allow this book's light to shine. It has been thoughtfully created in meditative prayer for your benefit and growth. I trust that you will treasure its wisdom and share it with those who would benefit from it.

Each day of the year offers a unique message for reflection. As you contemplate this wisdom, I have paired it with biblical verses that provide deeper context on how to apply these insights. Therefore, it's recommended to read this book alongside the Holy Bible. This book is specifically designed for daily reading throughout the year, and you can start it on any day. The biblical passages are of utmost importance, and you may notice key verses repeated throughout. A vital lesson is that any life situation can be connected to scriptural teachings. It brings immense joy to know that God's Holy Word can guide you through your journey. When in doubt, rely on the truths found in God's Word.

We are all uniquely created by God. As Saint Carlo Acutis wisely stated, "All people are born as originals, but many die as photocopies." Embrace your gifts and live fully in joy, love, and kindness, just as God intends for you. Seek the wisdom that will support both you and others on your journey. Always remember that you are never alone. Among all the experiences I've had in life, I cherish being your faithful godfather as my greatest accomplishment. May the Holy Spirit continue to bless and guide you throughout your life.

JANUARY 1

Accept Jesus Christ as your savior and make Him Lord over everything in your life.

How: Romans 10:9–10; Galatians 2:20

_____

_____

_____

JANUARY 2

When asked about your greatest accomplishment, consider responding with, "My most recent act of kindness." Utilize your talents to support and uplift others.

How: Ephesians 4:32; Colossians 3:12; Proverbs 19:17

_____

_____

_____

JANUARY 3

Health encompasses a spectrum that includes the mind, body, spirit, emotions, and financial well-being. To achieve a truly healthy body, it is essential to nurture and enrich all these aspects of health.

How: Jeremiah 33:6; 1 Corinthians 6:19–20; Exodus 23:25

_____

_____

_____

JANUARY 4

Alcohol, caffeine, and sugar can distance you from realizing your full potential. It's essential to engage with these substances with great care.

How: 1 Corinthians 6:12; Proverbs 23:1–3

_____

_____

_____

JANUARY 5

Read as many books as possible. It's more beneficial to learn from the mistakes of others than to make them yourself. Keep in mind Mark Twain's insight: "The man who doesn't read good books has no advantage over the man who can't read them."

How: Proverbs 1:5; 2 Timothy 3:16–17; Proverbs 4:7

_____

_____

_____

JANUARY 6

Identify your values early on and hold steadfast to them. Let them guide you in every decision and action you take.

How: Micah 6:8; Proverbs 4:23

_____

_____

_____

JANUARY 7

I once had dinner with Peter Schwartz at Salesforce. He is the author of *The Art of the Long View*. I asked him to sign my copy of the book and to inscribe a piece of wisdom he wished he had known in his youth. He wrote, "If it doesn't take fifty years, it's not worth doing. For our shared future."

How: Proverbs 10:4; Proverbs 13:4; Colossians 3:23

_____

_____

_____

JANUARY 8

Upon entering the workforce, choose a role that allows you to earn equity (stock). This approach fosters faster wealth accumulation. While bonuses and annual raises can fluctuate, equity has the potential for significant long-term growth.

How: Proverbs 13:11; Ecclesiastes 11:2

_____

_____

_____

JANUARY 9

Never cheat! While it may provide temporary satisfaction, it will lead to long-term pain and suffering.

How: Proverbs 6:16–19; Proverbs 12:22

_____

_____

_____

JANUARY 10

Become skilled at recognizing distractions. The energy you invest in these diversions keeps you from realizing your full potential. In today's world, social media and excessive screen time represent some of the most significant distractions.

How: Proverbs 4:25–27; Luke 10:38–42

_____

_____

_____

JANUARY 11

Make it a daily practice to pray and study the Bible. By doing so, you will find answers to all your questions. God responds to your prayers in one of three ways:
1. Yes.
2. Yes, but not at this moment.
3. No, I have a better plan for you.

How: Psalm 119:105; Joshua 1:8

_____

_____

_____

JANUARY 12

Always dedicate your time and energy to your friendships. Don't allow life's challenges to hinder your relationships, whether with friends or in your marriage. As you age, the significance of having friends who have known you since your youth becomes increasingly important.

How: Proverbs 18:24; Ecclesiastes 4:9–10

_____

_____

_____

JANUARY 13

Strive for excellence in all your endeavors. While this journey may not be easy, it demands energy, discipline, focus, commitment, intelligence, action, and even enjoyment! The rewards of such dedication far outweigh the sacrifices made. Remember, it's essential to avoid lingering in any organization that does not prioritize excellence.

How: Colossians 3:23; Ecclesiastes 9:10

JANUARY 14

Embrace the qualities of kindness, joy, and love in your spirit. As you navigate through life, you will face various challenges. Remember that even in the toughest moments, a little more kindness, love, and joy can make a significant difference.

How: 1 Corinthians 13:4; Galatians 5:22; Romans 12:10

JANUARY 15

The Dark Room Full of Anger and Hate

The door to this room is always open
It's open when your argument fails logic
It's open when you don't understand
It's open to judgment
It's open to intolerance
It's open to violence
It welcomes your fear
It encourages dehumanization
It hardens the heart
It discourages knowledge
It loves name calling
It loves to cancel people

It truly is Hell on Earth

How: Matthew 5:44; Leviticus 19:18; Proverbs 10:12

_____

_____

_____

JANUARY 16

Attend church and pray, even if you're not inclined to do so. Open yourself up to the Holy Spirit and let Him fulfill God's purpose within you.

How: Hebrews 10:25; Acts 2:42

JANUARY 17

Always arrive early to meetings and come prepared. Avoid improvising. Your time is your most valuable resource, and if you're dedicating it to a meeting, you deserve to bring your best effort.

How: Matthew 24:42–44; Proverbs 6:6–8

JANUARY 18

Make it a priority to walk outdoors in nature every day. Some of my most creative ideas have come to me during these walks. Beethoven, for instance, would take daily strolls in the woods, finding both inspiration and peace in his surroundings. His deep appreciation for the countryside is reflected in his 6th Symphony, the "Pastoral."

How: Psalm 19:1–4; Isaiah 55:12; Psalm 104

JANUARY 19

Fear and doubt are natural aspects of life. There will be times when it feels like negative thoughts are overwhelming you. During these moments, try to shift your focus toward gratitude. Remember, there is always someone who would willingly exchange their circumstances for yours.

How: Philippians 4:8; 1 Peter 5:7; Proverbs 4:23

JANUARY 20

Always exhibit good manners. Stand up when greeting someone, and remember to shake hands while maintaining eye contact. Use polite responses such as "Yes, sir" and "Yes, ma'am." It's thoughtful to send thank-you notes. Men should stand when a lady enters or exits the room and offer assistance when people are being seated. Lastly, consider marrying someone who embodies these same values.

How: 1 Peter 3:8; Matthew 7:12

JANUARY 21

Explore classic literature to uncover the timeless wisdom it offers. Engaging with these texts will not only enrich your understanding of the world but also enhance your critical reasoning skills, which are crucial in today's society.

How: 1 Thessalonians 5:21; Proverbs 4:7

JANUARY 22

Listen with the intent to understand rather than to respond. Even if you believe you grasp the concept, inquire further for a deeper understanding.

How: James 1:19–20; Proverbs 18:13; Luke 11:28

JANUARY 23

Take care of your appearance by being clean and well-dressed. This reflects respect for both yourself and those around you. Remember, you are a sacred temple for the Lord.

How: 1 Corinthians 3:16; Isaiah 1:16

JANUARY 24

Pray with humility and dedication on your knees. Show reverence to God in everything you do.

How: Psalms 95:6; Hebrews 12:28–29; Psalm 2:11

_____

_____

_____

JANUARY 25

Everything you accomplish will never come close to the joy of kindness.

How: John 13:34

_____

_____

_____

JANUARY 26

The present moment is all you truly possess. How you choose to respond to it is influenced by your faith, values, intellect, and love.

How: Matthew 6:34; Ephesians 5:16

JANUARY 27

Always be aware of when and how to adapt. As Mike Tyson famously stated, "Everyone has a plan until they get hit in the face."

How: Romans 12:2; Psalm 46:1; 2 Corinthians 4:8–9

JANUARY 28

At times in life, you may give your all and strive for greatness, yet still fall short. Regardless, continue to embody a person of excellence.

How: Proverbs 24:16; Romans 5:3–5

_____

_____

_____

JANUARY 29

Everyone seeks excellence, yet many are unwilling to invest the effort necessary to attain it.

How: Hebrews 12:6; Proverbs 25:28; Proverbs 12:1

_____

_____

_____

JANUARY 30

Allocate equal time to understanding your audience as you do to crafting your presentation or pitch. Many individuals focus solely on developing their content.

How: Acts 17; Colossians 4:6; Ephesians 4:29

_____

_____

_____

JANUARY 31

One day, you will encounter someone who is likely to be either older or much younger than you. They will not be interested in your material possessions, job title, physical prowess, intellect, social status, or circle of friends. It is during that moment that you may realize the true extent of your poverty. Remember to be kind!

How: Matthew 6:19–21; Luke 12:15

_____

_____

_____

FEBRUARY 1

Live by the Scout Law: Trustworthy, Loyal, Helpful, Friendly, Courteous, Kind, Obedient, Cheerful, Thrifty, Brave, Clean, and Reverent. The last is most important!

How: Proverbs 19:22; I Corinthians 4:1–2; Matthew 25:35–36; John 15:12–13; 1 Peter 3:8; Ephesians 4:32; Hebrews 13:17; Proverbs 17:22; Proverbs 28:27; 2 Timothy 1:7; Psalm 51:10; Proverbs 19:23

_____

_____

_____

FEBRUARY 2

The Army Ranger Creed is how you are to approach every situation in life!

"Recognizing that I volunteered as a Ranger, fully knowing the hazards of my chosen profession, I will always endeavor to uphold the prestige, honor, and high esprit de corps of the Rangers.

"Acknowledging the fact that a Ranger is a more elite Soldier who arrives at the cutting edge of battle by land, sea, or air, I accept the fact that as a Ranger my country expects me to move further, faster, and fight harder than any other Soldier.

"Never shall I fail my comrades. I will always keep myself mentally alert, physically strong, and morally straight, and I will shoulder more than my share of the task whatever it may be, one hundred percent and then some.

"Gallantly will I show the world that I am a specially selected and well-trained Soldier. My courtesy to superior officers, neatness of dress, and care of equipment shall set the example for others to follow.

"Energetically will I meet the enemies of my country. I shall defeat them on the field of battle for I am better trained and will fight with all my might. Surrender is not a Ranger word. I will never leave a fallen comrade to fall into the hands of the enemy and under no circumstances will I ever embarrass my country.

"Readily will I display the intestinal fortitude required to fight on to the Ranger objective and complete the mission though I be the lone survivor.

"Rangers lead the way!"

How: Psalm 144:1–2; Psalm 91; 2 Timothy 2:4

_____

_____

_____

FEBRUARY 3

The three most impactful letters in the alphabet are N, O, W. Don't allow the past or the future to diminish their significance.

How: Matthew 6:34; Psalm 118:24

_____

_____

_____

FEBRUARY 4

Make it a habit to read and reread the Bible each day. True wisdom unfolds within its pages. Even after reading certain passages a hundred times, I continue to discover new insights.

How: Psalm 1

_____

_____

_____

FEBRUARY 5

Every morning presents a choice: to acknowledge and appreciate what you have or to be overwhelmed by what you lack. The wiser option is to choose gratitude.

How: Psalm 95; Psalm 100:4; James 1:17

_____

_____

_____

FEBRUARY 6

Always show kindness and offer assistance to those who may never be able to repay you. While people might forget the specific actions you've taken for them, they will always remember how you made them feel.

How: Ephesians 4:32; Acts 20:35

_____

_____

_____

FEBRUARY 7

Be swift to forgive. We all miss the mark when it comes to living up to God's glory, even when others are at fault. Holding onto resentment only harms you.

How: Colossians 3:13; Mark 11:25; James 5:16

_____

_____

_____

FEBRUARY 8

Be aware of the company you choose to surround yourself with. Each group of people has its own lessons to offer. Some individuals uplift and empower you, while others may diminish your strength. Recognize this distinction and respond to those who challenge you with compassion and prayers for their growth.

How: Proverbs 13:20; 1 Corinthians 15:33–34

_____

_____

_____

FEBRUARY 9

Honor the people you love by your actions.

How: Proverbs

_____

_____

_____

FEBRUARY 10

Numerous individuals have made sacrifices to help you reach your current position. This includes not only your immediate family but also soldiers, priests, educators, chefs, police officers, politicians, scientists, doctors, musicians, and many others.

How: 1 Timothy 6:17–19; Proverbs 21:26; 2 Corinthians 9:11

_____

_____

_____

FEBRUARY 11

Everyone has different values, and that's what makes each of us unique. When searching for a life partner, seek out the values that complement and enhance your own, and vice versa. Think of it as a harmonious duet: you both share a love for music, but while you play the violin, your partner plays the cello. Together, you create a beautiful melody that you couldn't achieve alone.

How: Proverbs 31:10; Matthew 19:5

_____

_____

_____

FEBRUARY 12

In matters of food, simplicity is key. Always express gratitude with a loud and heartfelt grace before every meal. Take your time to enjoy each bite and avoid overindulging in treats.

How: Proverbs 23:20–21; Matthew 4:4

FEBRUARY 13

We have entered an Information Age in which it is practically impossible for any individual to stay abreast of the latest innovations. It is crucial to critically examine data, sources, mathematical models, and potential biases.

How: 1 Thessalonians 5:21; Proverbs 1:1–33; Luke 14:28

FEBRUARY 14

Not everyone is open to learning during an argument. In such cases, it may be more effective to disengage. Those who lack insight often don't ask questions; they merely respond based on their limited perspective.

How: Proverbs 23:9; Proverbs 26:4

_____

_____

_____

FEBRUARY 15

You are not defined by your accomplishments; rather, you are defined by your kindness. Kindness toward all living beings, kindness toward those who may never be able to repay you, and kindness toward those you support and uplift.

How: John 13:34–35

_____

_____

_____

FEBRUARY 16

Never sacrifice your principles in pursuit of wealth, power, or popularity. Doing so will ultimately lead to your downfall.

How: Ephesians 6:10–11; 2 Timothy 1:7; Deuteronomy 31:6

_____

_____

_____

FEBRUARY 17

Treasure and value the friendships you form in your early years. As you grow older, having friends who have known you since your youth becomes increasingly significant.

How: Sirach 6:14–17

_____

_____

_____

FEBRUARY 18

As you grow more accomplished and skilled, it may become increasingly difficult to discern the truth. People will often inundate you with flattery in hopes of gaining your approval.

How: Ephesians 4:25; 1 Thessalonians 5:21; James 1:5–6

FEBRUARY 19

When choosing a spouse, it's important to closely observe their family dynamics, as this process requires time and careful consideration. The way a family interacts can significantly indicate future happiness in your relationship. Pay attention to the details: Do family members treat one another with respect? Is there a sense of love among them? Are they generally happy?

How: Matthew 7:16; Proverbs 24:27; Ephesians 5:22–33

FEBRUARY 20

It's crucial to have a partner who values an active lifestyle. This goes beyond simply competing in sports; it's about dedicating oneself to maintaining a disciplined approach to health for both yourself and your family. Embracing physical wellness not only enhances physical well-being but also fosters mental and spiritual growth.

How: 1 Corinthians 6:19–20; 1 Timothy 4:8

_____

_____

_____

FEBRUARY 21

Everyone thinks they will be able to earn an income after age fifty. Invest early on in life so you don't have to depend on a job after age fifty.

How: Proverbs 21:20; Proverbs 13:11; Proverbs 21:5

_____

_____

_____

FEBRUARY 22

Explore the world while you're young. Venture off the beaten path to experience diverse cultures to the fullest.

How: Mark 16:15; Deuteronomy 31:8

FEBRUARY 23

One of the most insightful ways to gauge a person's character is by playing a round of golf with them, particularly if they are not an experienced player. Through observing their adherence to the rules, you can assess their trustworthiness. You'll also notice how they handle challenges, revealing their resilience and emotional control. Their level of courtesy and respect for the game, fellow players, and the course itself will be evident. Moreover, their enjoyment of the game will reflect their joyful spirit. Lastly, their choice of club and approach to a swing can indicate whether they are strategic thinkers or more inclined to take risks.

How: Philippians 4:8; James 2:14–26; Proverbs 24:16

FEBRUARY 24

Learn to play chess; it enhances your strategic thinking skills.

How: Proverbs 24:6; Proverbs 15:22

_____

_____

_____

FEBRUARY 25

Learn to play poker, as it also sharpens your strategic thinking abilities. Additionally, it helps you focus on reading opponents rather than merely considering the cards in your hand.

How: Proverbs 23:5; Proverbs 4:7; Proverbs 18:15

_____

_____

_____

FEBRUARY 26

Make sure to maintain eye contact when you ask someone a question. If their eyes shift to the left, they are likely remembering past experiences. Conversely, if their eyes move to the right, they are probably creating or envisioning something that hasn't occurred yet.

How: Proverbs 6:16–19; Proverbs 12:19; Ephesians 4:25

_____

_____

_____

FEBRUARY 27

Regulate your thoughts and actions and avoid becoming a prisoner of their power over you. Many circumstances and virtually all interpersonal interactions lie outside your control.

How: Romans 8:28; Psalm 37:5

_____

_____

_____

FEBRUARY 28

There will be moments of profound sadness in life. It's important not to succumb to negative thoughts during these times. I've found that a good night's sleep can often shift your perspective by morning. If feelings of sorrow persist, take a moment to reflect on the lessons you might be learning from the experience. Then, consider how you can change your thoughts, actions, or circumstances to foster a more positive outlook.

How: Psalm 34:18; Romans 8:18; John 16:22

_____

_____

_____

FEBRUARY 29 LEAP YEAR

Life will bring you moments of immense joy. It's important to remember how beautiful it is to share these experiences with others. At the heart of great joy, you will always discover a love for others.

How: Romans 12:15; Galatians 5:22; 1 Timothy 6:18

_____

_____

_____

MARCH 1

When offering compliments or writing thank-you notes, sincerity is key. Take the time to craft something unique. People will always remember how you made them feel.

How: 1 Thessalonians 5:18; Psalm 107:1

_____

_____

_____

MARCH 2

Engage with your elders. Question them deeply to truly comprehend, rather than simply to reply. The most profound wisdom resides in those who are sixty years and older. Neglecting their insights can lead you to repeat past mistakes, while embracing their knowledge can lead to new opportunities.

How: Leviticus 19:32; 1 Timothy 5:1–2; 1 Peter 5:5

_____

_____

_____

MARCH 3

Social media has become one of the most potent forms of addiction. It manipulates the brain's primitive regions to maintain user engagement. Additionally, it creates the illusion of having many friends. However, nothing compares to the experience of connecting with others in person.

How: Hebrews 10:24–25; Romans 12:10; 1 Thessalonians 5:11

MARCH 4

Select your friends and colleagues thoughtfully, as they mirror who you are. Surround yourself with individuals who challenge and inspire you with their intelligence. While it's important to embrace diversity, ensure it aligns with your core values.

How: Proverbs 12:26; Proverbs 13:20; Daniel 12:3

MARCH 5

You have two options: invest $10 a day in McDonald's stock (MCD) or spend $10 daily on their products. If you choose to invest, it would take around thirty years to accumulate a $1 million portfolio, assuming an average annual return of 7%. Don't take the easy road!

How: Proverbs 13:11; Proverbs 21:5; Proverbs 24:27

MARCH 6

Gym memberships, bottled water, premium coffee, video games, and streaming services will drain your finances. Be frugal with your savings, but invest generously in the pursuit of knowledge and acts of kindness. These pursuits are everlasting and are treasured in heaven.

How: Proverbs 21:20; Luke 12:21

MARCH 7

Revisit your favorite books. The key to life lies in continuous learning, relearning, and unlearning.

How: Proverbs 1:5; Proverbs 9:9

_____

_____

_____

MARCH 8

People typically don't take risks with the expectation of gaining something; instead, they often take risks when they anticipate a potential loss. This perspective is crucial to keep in mind when making any requests.

How: Ecclesiastes 11:4–6; Matthew 14:28–29; Proverbs 22:3

_____

_____

_____

MARCH 9

Intermittent reinforcement refers to a reward schedule in which a desired behavior is rewarded sporadically, rather than consistently. This unpredictability can create a strong sense of anticipation, making it highly engaging. For individuals engaging in the behavior, the occasional reward encourages them to put in extra effort to achieve it. To minimize repetitive nagging, ensure that your affirmatives and negatives are clear and decisive.

How: Matthew 5:37

_____

_____

_____

MARCH 10

Impulsive decisions rarely result in positive outcomes. They often stem from the primal part of the brain responsible for survival instincts. It's beneficial to take a moment to pause and reflect before making any choice.

How: Genesis 25:29–34; Proverbs 14:17; Numbers 20:7–12

_____

_____

_____

MARCH 11

The individual who exudes the highest level of confidence in a room is often the one with the least intelligence. This phenomenon is a clear example of the Dunning-Kruger effect, which is prevalent in various settings. It's important to critically evaluate those who display excessive confidence or claim to possess high levels of competence.

How: Proverbs 16:18; James 4:6; Philippians 2:3

_____

_____

_____

MARCH 12

Always remember three types of people: those who abandoned you in your struggles, those who supported you during tough times, and those who contributed to your hardships. Each of these moments reveals true character. Both good times and bad times are fleeting, but character is enduring.

How: The book of Job

_____

_____

_____

MARCH 13

Always strive to give your utmost in every endeavor. You never know when your final opportunity will arise. True excellence cannot be attained through half-hearted efforts.

How: Colossians 3:23–24; Daniel 6:3

_____

_____

_____

MARCH 14

As you deepen your knowledge, the significance of meditation increases. Aim to practice one to two sessions of twenty minutes each daily, especially during stressful periods. A tranquil mind leads to improved results.

How: Psalm 119:15; Psalm 77:12; Psalm 1:2

_____

_____

_____

MARCH 15

Be kind to yourself. Don't allow a mistake to occupy your mind unnecessarily. Recognize it, learn from it, and then release it. Avoid letting the past or future take away from your present moment.

How: Matthew 11:28–30; 1 Peter 5:7; Proverbs 17:22

_____

_____

_____

MARCH 16

Whenever you're feeling burdened by anxiety, negativity, or sadness, take a moment to jot down your thoughts. Reflect on how these thoughts affect your emotions and the consequences they produce. Next, envision how you would feel if you could let go of these thoughts. This straightforward practice helps retrain your brain to break free from unproductive patterns and recognize the benefits of releasing limiting beliefs. From a scientific perspective, this approach leverages the brain's capacity to rewire itself in response to new experiences and habits.

How: Joshua 1:9; Psalm 42:11

_____

_____

_____

MARCH 17

Lessons I've Gained from Focusing on My Physical Health: When I'm tired, hungry, or juggling multiple tasks, I tend to make more mistakes and allow my emotions to take over. I've experienced this firsthand while playing chess; I notice that when I'm not at my physical best, I struggle to identify winning moves.

How: Matthew 11:28; Psalm 37:7; Hebrews 4:11

_____

_____

_____

MARCH 18

To achieve optimal physical performance, it's essential to maintain a balance among sleep, nutrition, and exercise. Many individuals tend to focus on just one of these elements at the expense of the others.

How: 1 Timothy 4:8; Isaiah 40:31

_____

_____

_____

MARCH 19

The most genuine and influential leaders prioritize real-world interactions over social media engagement. Your online posts may inadvertently contribute to keeping others glued to their screens, preventing them from fully experiencing life around them. Consider reducing your social media activity and share insights only when needed, encouraging others to connect with the world beyond their devices.

How: Mark 12:30–31; Ephesians 5:16; Galatians 5:22–23

MARCH 20

Good manners are a way to honor your parents. They demonstrate your respect for both others and yourself.

How: 1 Peter 3:8; Matthew 7:12

MARCH 21

Honoring our veterans is essential! When you encounter them in a restaurant, consider anonymously covering their meal. Engage in acts of kindness without expecting anything in return to brighten their lives. Remember, they served for our benefit!

How: 2 Timothy 2:3–4; Romans 8:38–39

_____

_____

_____

MARCH 22

Spend quiet moments in the presence of God. Keep in mind that His voice is gentle and soft, often conveyed in whispers rather than in loud proclamations.

How: 1 Kings 19:11–13

_____

_____

_____

MARCH 23

Embark on a remarkable adventure with your parents. I had the pleasure of experiencing the Passion Play in Oberammergau, Germany, with my mother, and exploring Scotland with my dad. It's a gift that rewards both them and yourself, creating lasting memories that continue to enrich your lives.

How: Exodus 20:12; Ephesians 6:2–3; Matthew 15:4

_____

_____

_____

MARCH 24

Fish are found in every corner of the globe. Instead of sticking to your favorite fishing spot, consider exploring new locations for the ultimate adventure.

How: Isaiah 43:18–19; Psalm 115:16

_____

_____

_____

MARCH 25

Avoid wasting time on fleeting distractions. True fulfillment comes from valuing the limited time we have and living purposefully for God.

How: Ephesians 5:15–16; 1 Timothy 4:7–11; Psalm 90:12

MARCH 26

One of the most meaningful ways to honor someone is by offering a heartfelt and genuine prayer for them. Similarly, the greatest way to honor God is by extending that same sentiment to someone who has wronged you.

How: Colossians 1:9–14; 1 Thessalonians 5:25; James 5:16

MARCH 27

Make all life decisions with careful consideration and thoughtfulness. For major choices, let your heart guide you; for simpler ones, rely on your intellect. Avoid wasting time on regrets after a decision has been made. Once you've committed to a choice, focus on improving the situation.

How: Jeremiah 29:11; Proverbs 16:3; Psalm 37:5

_____

_____

_____

MARCH 28

Music is a wonderful gift from God. St. Augustine is known for saying, "To sing is to pray twice." It's important to choose your music carefully, as not all songs uplift the spirit.

How: Psalm 150; Psalm 98:5; Colossians 3:16

_____

_____

_____

MARCH 29

Make it a habit to journal each day—not merely to document daily occurrences but to reflect on them with gratitude. This practice will enhance your writing skills, elevate your mood, and help you cultivate a mindset focused on possibilities.

How: Habakkuk 2:2; Jeremiah 30:2

_____

_____

_____

MARCH 30

Always look for opportunities to collaborate with others. Each person brings unique perspectives that can enhance any idea. The music of Paul McCartney and John Lennon was far more impactful when they worked together than when they pursued solo careers.

How: Ecclesiastes 4:9–12; Romans 15:5–6

_____

_____

_____

MARCH 31

Avoid associating with those who do not believe in Jesus Christ. Instead, pray for them and let your actions serve as a testament to the Gospel. Approach them with gentleness, respect, and courage, rather than timidity.

How: 2 Corinthians 6:14; Proverbs 22:24–25

_____

_____

_____

APRIL 1

Always be ready to share your testimony of faith in Jesus Christ. Present it with compassion, respect, and bravery, for you may never know when the Holy Spirit prompts you to help guide someone else's soul to salvation.

How: Matthew 10:32; Revelation 12:11; Psalm 71:15–16

_____

_____

_____

APRIL 2

Always continue to deepen your understanding of your faith. Explore the foundational texts of your religion and immerse yourself in daily Bible study. Visit Jerusalem and walk the paths where Jesus Christ once tread. Discover the lives of the saints and what distinguished them.

How: John 17:3; Hebrews 4:12; 2 Peter 3:18

_____

_____

_____

APRIL 3

Avoid using drugs that impair your natural cognitive abilities. Engaging in such behavior offers no benefits and leads to significant losses.

How: 1 Corinthians 10:13; Proverbs 20:1

_____

_____

_____

APRIL 4

Every type of work holds inherent dignity, whether it is intellectually challenging or physically demanding. This includes tasks that are unpaid. Put forth your best effort in all that you do, as it brings respect not only to others but also to yourself.

How: Proverbs 14:23; Colossians 3:23–24

_____

_____

_____

APRIL 5

All prayer is good. Instead of treating it as a routine, approach God with an open heart, filled with reverence and humility. When you do so, He will genuinely respond to your prayers.

How: 1 Thessalonians 5:17; Philippians 4:6

_____

_____

_____

APRIL 6

When studying individuals or organizations, it's important to grasp the reason behind their actions before inquiring about the "what" or "how." If their fundamental purpose, or "why," is not aligned, then their methods and objectives become irrelevant.

How: Matthew 7:15–20; Proverbs 20:5

_____

_____

_____

APRIL 7

It's normal to feel nervous before a significant event. To calm your nerves, find a quiet space, close your eyes, and take five minutes to breathe deeply. Additionally, take a moment to pray to God for guidance and support.

How: Philippians 4:6–7, 1 Peter 5:7

_____

_____

_____

APRIL 8

You might have achieved something remarkable, or perhaps you haven't. The most daunting part isn't establishing the goal; it's reaching it. You'll discover that what once appeared unattainable was actually within your grasp. Did you push yourself to your fullest potential?

How: Philippians 3:14; Philippians 3:13

_____

_____

_____

APRIL 9

You are invaluable to God; there has never been, nor will there ever be, anyone quite like you. You are a unique masterpiece crafted by God.

How: Jeremiah 1:5

_____

_____

_____

APRIL 10

Just as life is filled with significant achievements, it also brings notable disappointments. Embrace these setbacks rather than fear them; they offer valuable lessons. When you experience them, you'll discover that those moments are often less daunting than you imagined. The anxieties we conjure in our minds tend to be more intimidating than the actual situations.

How: Proverbs 24:16; James 1:2–4

APRIL 11

For my Eagle Scout project in 1986, I painted a mile of fence. Through this experience, I discovered several important lessons: People are eager to join you at the beginning of a big endeavor, but many will drift away as the project continues. It's essential to maintain your faith during the challenging moments when you feel isolated. Ultimately, the rewards at the end will make the struggles worthwhile.

How: Hebrews 12:1; Romans 5:3–4; Revelation 2:3

APRIL 12

Throughout my years of competitive long-distance running, I adopted a strategy of sprinting at full speed for an additional ten seconds whenever I overtook another runner. Even in moments of exhaustion, this tactic ensured that no one was able to pass me. I realized that the mind often gives up before the body does; if you push your mental limits, your body will follow.

How: Philippians 2:3–4; 1 Corinthians 9:24; 2 Timothy 2:5

_____

_____

_____

APRIL 13

Quitting becomes easier with each instance, ultimately leading you to a path of regret and sorrow.

How: Galatians 6:9; Hebrews 10:35–36

_____

_____

_____

APRIL 14

The most potent drug in the world is comfort! In this space, nothing thrives. You become slower, heavier, and less sharp. Be cautious about accumulating possessions in pursuit of comfort.

How: Proverbs 19:15; 2 Thessalonians 3:10; Proverbs 13:4

APRIL 15

Avoid making judgments about people. However, if you must, assess them based on their questions and how they buy a Porterhouse steak from the butcher.

How: Proverbs 18:15; 1 Thessalonians 5:21

APRIL 16

Breakthroughs, innovation, and creativity seldom arise under pressure. Instead, they often emerge during moments of play, free from the constraints of time, or in periods of relaxation when your most brilliant ideas take shape.

How: Ephesians 2:10; Colossians 3:23

_____

_____

_____

APRIL 17

Would you prefer to have your phone in your hand or another person's hand in your hand during life's most significant moments? You can choose only one. Reflect on what truly matters to you.

How: Hebrews 10:24–25; Acts 2:42–47; Ephesians 4:32

_____

_____

_____

APRIL 18

When embracing a challenge, do so with joy and kindness in your heart. A negative attitude only complicates matters for yourself and those around you.

How: Philippians 4:8; Psalm 139:23–24; 2 Corinthians 10:5

_____

_____

_____

APRIL 19

You can tolerate more physical stress than you might think. To illustrate, in 2019, I finished twelfth in my age group at the Zofingen Powerman World Championship, a grueling nine-hour cycling and running race in the Swiss Alps. The conditions were brutal, with freezing temperatures and rain. There were countless moments when I felt like giving up. However, I pushed through by concentrating on small victories—whether it was completing one more climb or finishing another lap. This approach helped me avoid feeling overwhelmed by the challenge ahead.

How: James 1:12; Ephesians 6:18

_____

_____

_____

APRIL 20

Discover your ancestry while you're still young. There's nothing quite like hearing about your family's experiences directly from your grandparents. Make the most of the time you have with them! I cherished the tales my grandmother told about our family's bravery during the American Revolutionary War. When I turned fifty-two, I took the time to verify her stories and proudly became a member of the Sons of the American Revolution.

How: Leviticus 19:32; Job 12:12; Proverbs 23:22

APRIL 21

Make sure to take an annual trip with your closest friends. It brings immense joy and creates some of your most cherished memories.

How: Proverbs 18:24; Proverbs 13:20; Job 6:14

APRIL 22

You truly realize how quickly life passes when you hit your fifties. Make sure to spend your time pursuing your own dreams instead of living someone else's.

How: Philippians 4:13; Jeremiah 29:11

APRIL 23

It's never too late to begin anew. Many of the most remarkable success stories emerged when individuals believed they were at the end of their road.

How: Isaiah 43:18–19; Lamentations 3:22–23

APRIL 24

I have experienced both riches and wealth. However, riches do not always equate to true wealth. For instance, riches represent the material possessions that individuals strive for throughout their lives. In contrast, wealth encompasses the diverse array of experiences and insights—like the various wildflowers we've encountered along the way. While riches can vanish in an instant, true wealth endures throughout one's life.

How: Luke 12:27–28; 2 Corinthians 9:8; Jeremiah 17:7–8

_____

_____

_____

APRIL 25

Do not let fear of anyone or anything govern your life. Face adversity with courage, knowing that the Lord Jesus Christ is always by your side, providing strength and support.

How: Isaiah 41:10; Joshua 1:9; Philippians 4:6–7; Psalm 23:4; Deuteronomy 31:6; Proverbs 1:7

_____

_____

_____

APRIL 26

Your gifts are meant to be shared with others. Share your talents joyfully and with an open heart. Charity brings hope to those who need it most.

How: 1 Peter 4:10–11; Romans 12:6–8; Hebrews 13:16; Luke 14:12–14

APRIL 27

Don't share your knowledge without charge; its worth diminishes in the wrong environment. Always inquire about how someone intends to apply your insights.

How: Proverbs 11:9; Hosea 4:6; Proverbs 18:15

APRIL 28

Make a point to write legibly. In today's digital age, a well-hand-written note can have a significant impact. It showcases your courtesy and professionalism.

How: Luke 1:3; Habakkuk 2:2; Matthew 13:51–52

_____

_____

_____

APRIL 29

If it doesn't require fifty years of effort, it's not worth pursuing. We're striving for a shared and beautiful future.

How: Colossians 3:23–24; Philippians 3:13–14

_____

_____

_____

APRIL 30

In life, you can never predict when you might find yourself in the role of a caregiver or in need of one. Both scenarios are inevitable, and it's essential to approach each with love, compassion, and kindness.

How: Luke 10:30–37; James 2:14–17; Sirach 38:9

_____

_____

_____

MAY 1

As you rise within any organization, you'll find that your time becomes increasingly limited, which can lead to added stress. However, there's no need to worry. Focus on making decisive choices guided by your core values. This approach will help you steer clear of time-wasting pursuits and ensure that your energy is directed toward meaningful efforts.

How: Ephesians 5:15–16; Colossians 4:5; Ecclesiastes 3:1

_____

_____

_____

MAY 2

Men, if you're interested in pursuing a future partner, maintaining a tidy bathroom and home is essential. Women, make sure to choose a partner who values cleanliness in their living space. Trust me, this advice is effective!

How: 1 Timothy 3:4–5; Matthew 23:26

_____

_____

_____

MAY 3

You are precisely where you're meant to be at this moment. God is overseeing His plan for your life. Let me emphasize that: God is in control of His plan for you.

How: Jeremiah 29:11

_____

_____

_____

MAY 4

There are two days in the year that seem unreal: yesterday and tomorrow. Don't allow them to take away the value of what is real—right now.

How: Isaiah 43:18–19; Proverbs 19:20–21

_____

_____

_____

MAY 5

The most remarkable library in the world consists of the senior citizens among us. I have had the privilege of meeting individuals who fought in the Battle of the Bulge during World War II. Cherish the moments you spend with your elders.

How: Leviticus 19:32; 1 Timothy 5:1–2; 1 Peter 5:5

_____

_____

_____

MAY 6

There's never a perfect moment to have children with your spouse. Rather than trying to control parenthood according to your schedule, entrust it to God. Children are truly one of life's greatest blessings.

How: Genesis 1:28; Hebrews 11:11

_____

_____

_____

MAY 7

Donating blood is one of the most invaluable gifts you can offer. It has the power to save lives, and the extent of the recipient's gratitude is something you may never fully understand.

How: Mark 12:31; John 15:13

_____

_____

_____

MAY 8

Cultivate the habit of waking up early in the morning. Many successful individuals begin their day at 5 AM or even earlier.

How: Psalm 119:147; Psalm 5:3; Proverbs 6:9–11

MAY 9

Your sleep schedule and nutrition are essential for maintaining peak performance. Do not undermine these crucial restorative practices.

How: Psalm 127:2; 1 Corinthians 10:31

MAY 10

In every walk I've taken through nature, I've discovered something new. At times, the lessons come easily, while other days they require more effort. Regardless of the challenge, I remain open minded and maintain a heart full of gratitude.

How: 1 Thessalonians 5:18; Ephesians 5:20

MAY 11

At times, you may find yourself in an uncomfortable situation or location. Focus your energy on constructive actions. With a little time—such as twenty-four hours—your perspective will likely change. Reflect on the lessons you can glean from this experience.

How: 1 Thessalonians 5:18; Philippians 4:13; James 1:2–3

MAY 12

Your network is one of your most valuable assets. Continuously invest in it. Additionally, ensure your network remains dynamic by stratifying it; aim for a diverse range of individuals segmented by ten to fifteen years. Mentor the younger members to equip them for future leadership roles.

How: Proverbs 18:24; Ephesians 4:16; Hebrews 10:24–25

MAY 13

Exercise caution when entering the political arena. You may end up investing significant personal time and financial resources, often at the expense of your family life. Additionally, be prepared for your opponents to go to great lengths to undermine your reputation.

How: Romans 13:1–7; Proverbs 31:8–9; Deuteronomy 1:13–15

MAY 14

Familiarize yourself with the scriptures! Society will often attempt to redefine sin as compassion, utilizing various forms of human reasoning to rationalize its actions. It's important to recognize that there is a distinction between believing in God and obeying Him.

How: Deuteronomy 28:1–68; 1 Samuel 15:22

MAY 15

I don't dine at Chick-fil-A every day, but on the occasions that I do, Reverend Billy Graham is right there with me on the radio. Somehow, my meal becomes ten times more flavorful.

How: 1 Thessalonians 5:18; 1 Corinthians 10:30–31

MAY 16

While there are numerous religions, the path to Heaven is found solely through Jesus Christ. It's important to respect all faiths, but also to examine their doctrines in light of solid biblical teachings. Always be ready to share your personal testimony about Jesus.

How: John 14:6; 2 Timothy 3:16–17

MAY 17

"Do a Good Turn Daily" is the motto of the Boy Scouts of America, and it has served as a guiding principle in my life. Here are a few insights I've gained from this simple act:

1. Generosity knows no bounds; every kind gesture returns to you tenfold.
2. Acts of kindness can elevate your spirit on tough days.
3. Kindness inspires those around you.
4. It has the power to genuinely help those on the receiving end of your goodwill.

How: Hebrews 13:2

MAY 18

Keep in mind that God responds to your prayers in His own timing, not yours. At times, you might sense that God isn't hearing you, but that's not true. God is present with you at every moment.

How: Joshua 1:9; Deuteronomy 31:8

MAY 19

Explore, read, and commit to memory your favorite poems. One of my personal favorites is "Invictus." I've discovered that great poetry ignites your passions and enriches your life.

How: Psalm 19:1–4; Sirach 39:15–17

MAY 20

My all-time favorite athlete is Steve Prefontaine, celebrated as the greatest long-distance runner in history. During the 1972 Munich Olympics, he had a chance to compete for the bronze medal, but that simply wasn't sufficient for him; he aimed for nothing less than gold. What truly inspired people was not just his incredible strength, but also his remarkable courage.

How: 2 Timothy 1:7; Proverbs 3:5–6; Isaiah 41:10

MAY 21

Surround yourself with individuals who engage in discussions about ideas and potential. Limit your interactions with those who focus on gossip or talk about others.

How: Proverbs 13:20; Proverbs 12:26; Psalm 1:1–6

MAY 22

The condition of your body can significantly influence your mental and emotional well-being. This underscores the importance of maintaining your physical health. When your mental or emotional state is not at its best, the quality of your decisions tends to suffer.

How: Proverbs 17:22; 1 Corinthians 6:19–20

_____

_____

_____

MAY 23

Always hold off on littering! Those who litter often lack impulse control and show a disregard for the environment, themselves, and those around them. Moreover, make it a point to properly dispose of any litter you encounter. Your efforts demonstrate consideration for others and a commitment to protecting our planet.

How: Psalm 24:1; Matthew 7:12

_____

_____

_____

MAY 24

Earn your wealth before turning fifty, then allow your money to generate returns for you afterward.

How: Proverbs 13:11; Proverbs 21:5; Proverbs 10:4

_____

_____

_____

MAY 25

Here are the types of individuals you should steer clear of: negative, untrustworthy, unkind, impatient, lustful, lazy, dishonest, self-centered, unfriendly, disorganized, unkempt, gossipy, gluttonous, greedy, and heartless. These traits emanate from an evil source.

How: James 3:16; Proverbs 4:14–19; Psalms 119:115

_____

_____

_____

MAY 26

Seek out mentors from various fields throughout your life. There are invaluable lessons to be gained from areas outside your formal education. Frequently, embracing diverse perspectives can lead to genuine innovation.

How: Proverbs 1:5; Psalm 71:18; Proverbs 9:9

MAY 27

Invest in things that can never be taken from you. This includes your education, knowledge, faith, compassion and kindness toward others, and love.

How: Luke 10:42

MAY 28

Those who understand recognize that retirement can significantly impact one's vitality. Your talents and contributions were meant to be utilized for much longer than just 50 years. Continue to embrace and apply them every day throughout your life.

How: 1 Peter 4:10

_____

_____

_____

MAY 29

There are three categories of people in the world: those who can play the guitar, those who aspire to learn, and those who have purchased guitars but don't play them. Procrastination often leads to feelings of regret.

How: James 1:2–4; Galatians 6:9

_____

_____

_____

MAY 30

Throughout life, you'll inevitably encounter difficult individuals. I've discovered two important insights about them. First, they often thrive on the attention of others, whether it's one person or a group. Second, beneath their troubling behavior lies a wounded and sorrowful inner child.

How: Matthew 5:44; Luke 6:27–29

_____

_____

_____

MAY 31

A significant amount of energy is lost to anxiety. Worry steals our peace of mind. Remarkably, the phrase "Do not be afraid" appears in the Bible around 365 times.

How: 1 John 4:18; Isaiah 41:10; Psalm 23:

_____

_____

_____

JUNE 1

Always be ready to take immediate action in a medical emergency. It's essential to know CPR, the Heimlich maneuver, and be aware of the F.A.S.T. method for identifying strokes (Face, Arm, Speech, Time). Additionally, understanding how to apply a tourniquet is crucial. You can also gain valuable knowledge by taking a first aid course.

How: Isaiah 1:17; Nahum 1:7

JUNE 2

Cultivate the mindset of an artist. Today, as I strolled through the Ann Arbor Peony Garden, I was overwhelmed by the sheer joy of witnessing over a hundred peonies in full bloom. Words fall short in capturing the experience; it's something you truly have to see for yourself. An artist once envisioned this breathtaking beauty long before it blossomed into reality.

How: Matthew 6:28–29; Psalm 19:1

JUNE 3

Support the caregivers by paying attention to the ways they assist others. Look for opportunities to bring a little joy into their lives. This simple act of kindness can make a significant difference.

How: John 13:34–35; Hebrews 6:10; James 1:27

_____

_____

_____

JUNE 4

Some physical pain must simply be tolerated. It's important to understand your body's reactions to stress, which can be achieved through the study of physiology. There are two main types of pain: the pain of discipline and the pain of disappointment.

How: Philippians 4:13; James 1:2–4

_____

_____

_____

JUNE 5

Diversity, equality, and inclusion do not require you to abandon your own beliefs in order to accept those of others. It is important to honor your own heritage while also respecting that of others. We are called to treat our neighbors as we would like to be treated ourselves.

How: Matthew 22:37–39; Jude 1:3

JUNE 6

Places, people, and property will inevitably change, sometimes for the better and at other times for the worse. However, when they uphold a shared value system and intentionally integrate it into their actions, they can navigate these changes more positively.

How: Ecclesiastes 3:1; Romans 12:2

JUNE 7

Chess mirrors life. Each move reveals three key elements: your training (the past), your plans (the future), and your interactions with other pieces (the present). Many players act on impulse, reacting solely to external stimuli. Remember, not everyone possesses a strategy, a set of values, or an education.

How: Proverbs 24:3–4; Proverbs 11:14

JUNE 8

Many individuals experience a comparable journey upon acquiring wealth. Initially, they embark on a globe-trotting adventure. Next, after they grow weary of travel, they focus on achieving peak physical fitness. Subsequently, it's common for them to invest in a major purchase, such as a yacht. Ultimately, if they manage to navigate these indulgent pursuits, they often turn their attention to philanthropic endeavors. It becomes evident that material pursuits often fail to fulfill the deeper needs of the soul.

How: Proverbs 19:17; Luke 12:33; Hebrews 13:16

JUNE 9

The desire to share extraordinary moments on social media can be harmful. It's important to remain humble. Those who genuinely experience remarkable events often refrain from posting about them online.

How: Colossians 3:12–14

_____

_____

_____

JUNE 10

Avoid debating with someone lacking intelligence. It's an exhausting use of your energy, and victory is unlikely. If engagement is necessary, I've found that asking questions can guide them toward recognizing their mistakes.

How: 1 Corinthians 13:4; Proverbs 14:7–9; 2 Timothy 3:7

_____

_____

_____

JUNE 11

When it comes to exercise and sports, moderation is key. It's easy to become overly focused on pursuing specific goals. I have achieved remarkable feats in my own quest for physical excellence. Yet, there is a price to pay. It's important to reflect on whether the time and effort invested are truly worthwhile.

How: Galatians 5:23; Corinthians 9:27; Matthew 6:33

JUNE 12

You might be able to organize an incredible event, but you can't dictate how others will react to it. True happiness comes not from seeking to satisfy others, but from focusing on what you can control.

How: Proverbs 25:28; Galatians 5:23

JUNE 13

Embrace the quiet moments. God speaks to us in subtle whispers.

How: Psalm 46:10; Habakkuk 2:20; 1 Kings 19:12

JUNE 14

To achieve greatness, you must master your mind. Recently, a female high school athlete shattered every long-distance American record in 2025. She attributed her success to not placing the previous records on a pedestal, which allowed her to surpass them. Remember, do not impose limitations on your indomitable spirit.

How: Mark 10:27; Jeremiah 32:17; Job 42:2

JUNE 15

Brian May, the lead guitarist of the rock band Queen, holds a PhD in Astrophysics from Imperial College London. Your journey in life is as distinctive as you are. It's fascinating how seemingly unrelated fields can come together to produce something extraordinary.

How: Ephesians 2:10; Luke 1:37

JUNE 16

You are so much more than the photos you take with your phone. I've often found that taking photos incessantly is an addiction. It takes away from the present moment that can never truly be captured digitally.

How: Philippians 3:13–14; Jeremiah 1:5; Psalm 139:13–18

JUNE 17

When I was a child, my grandmother Elinor once told me, "You will never feel lonely with opera." At the time, I didn't fully grasp the meaning behind her words, but I came to appreciate them as I grew older. Every Sunday, she would listen to operas from the New York Metropolitan, immersing herself in the beauty of the art form. It's a treasure I encourage everyone to support and embrace as much as possible.

How: Psalms 95:1; James 5:13; Psalm 150:3–5

JUNE 18

Picture nurturing a dog with such abundant love that they believe each day is like waking up on Christmas morning. Love is not exclusive to humans; it extends to every living being and all the things we encounter.

How: Genesis 1:25; Psalm 50:10; Exodus 20:11

JUNE 19

When you encounter someone for the first time, take a moment to note something distinctive about them. Make it a practice to remember these little details. Additionally, consider reaching out to them from time to time with a kind word or gesture. This is a fantastic way to foster trust and strengthen your connections.

How: 1 Thessalonians 5:11; Proverbs 18:24

_____

_____

_____

JUNE 20

In high school, I was among the top runners in the nation, consistently finishing races well ahead of my competitors. Even during training sessions, I outpaced everyone around me. However, my mistake was not training or competing with the best athletes in the world. To truly reach an elite level, it's essential to surround yourself with individuals who are smarter and stronger than you.

How: Philippians 4:13; Romans 12:1–2

_____

_____

_____

JUNE 21

In 1939, George Dantzig, a graduate student at UC Berkeley, arrived twenty minutes late to his statistics class. To avoid disrupting anyone, he copied a math problem from the blackboard into his notebook, assuming it was his homework. After returning to his dormitory, he spent several days diligently working on the problem. Eventually, he arrived at a solution and submitted it to his professor. Unbeknownst to George, the problems written on the board were actually two unsolvable conundrums that had stumped the brightest minds in the field. Had he realized these problems were deemed impossible, he likely would not have attempted to solve them. This story serves as a powerful reminder: never limit yourself—anything is achievable.

How: Philippians 4:13; 1 Corinthians 10:13

JUNE 22

Always keep a supply of professional thank-you cards and stamps on hand. Make it a habit to write legible, handwritten notes to individuals who have supported you or demonstrated great courage. Taking the time to express your gratitude in this way makes a significant impact.

How: 1 Thessalonians 5:18; Colossians 3:17

JUNE 23

In life, you will have opportunities to join various groups and boards. Only consider joining organizations that make a meaningful contribution to charity. Your time is your most valuable asset. Keep in mind that charity starts at home, with your family.

How: Proverbs 19:17; Matthew 6:3–4; Hebrews 13:16

JUNE 24

Avoid joining an organization solely to boost your social status, including prestigious groups within the Ivy League. Such motivations may inflate your ego while diminishing genuine humility.

How: Proverbs 16:18; Romans 12:3; Proverbs 16:5

_____

_____

_____

JUNE 25

Effective communication across different cultures often leads to misunderstandings. It's essential to approach learning about other cultural groups with an open mind. What one person considers a gesture of kindness might be perceived as offensive by someone from another background.

How: Galatians 3:28; Deuteronomy 10:19; 1 Corinthians 12:12–30

_____

_____

_____

JUNE 26

Create a video recording featuring your parents or grandparents. Engage them in conversation by asking about their lives, aspirations, fears, and experiences of love. In the future, you will cherish this recording so deeply that it may bring you to tears.

How: Exodus 20:12; Proverbs 23:22; Matthew 19:19

_____

_____

_____

JUNE 27

Consider owning a stylish sports car, ensuring it features a manual transmission. A stick shift not only enhances your connection to the driving experience but also makes for a more enjoyable ride.

How: Ecclesiastes 5:19

_____

_____

_____

JUNE 28

The wisest individuals understand the importance of playing the long game. Top consulting firms recognize this and invest in developing client talent even before they reach executive positions. Therefore, focus on building your network with this perspective in mind.

How: Ecclesiastes 4:9–12; Proverbs 27:17

_____

_____

_____

JUNE 29

Upon waking each morning, take a moment to express gratitude to God. Next, offer a prayer for guidance to fulfill His will. Finally, rise and start pursuing your goals with enthusiasm.

How: Psalm 143:8; Lamentations 3:22–23

_____

_____

_____

JUNE 30

Request to join a game you've never tried before. You'll gain more insight into communication and culture in this experience than in any other activity.

How: Hebrews 13:2; Matthew 25:35

JULY 1

On this day in 2004, my mother lost her battle with cancer at the age of sixty-six. In the moments I spent with her before she passed, I was deeply touched by the gratitude she felt for the life she had lived. We never know when God will summon us home, so it's important to cherish each day as a precious gift from Him.

How: Romans 12:1–2; 1 Corinthians 10:31

JULY 2

External appearances can often be misleading. It's important to assess individuals based on their consistent actions. Without Jesus in their lives, no amount of material wealth can conceal their underlying pain.

How: Joel 2:13; Matthew 7:16

JULY 3

What is faith? Faith is the complete trust and confidence we place in our Lord and Savior, Jesus Christ, particularly when the journey before us challenges our human understanding and beliefs.

How: Hebrews 11:6; Matthew 21:22; Proverbs 3:5–6

JULY 4

America is one of the most remarkable places in the world. While it faces challenges due to its diverse population, it is essential to uphold your responsibility to defend the Constitution of the United States against all enemies, both foreign and domestic.

How: Psalm 33:12; Romans 13:1–7

JULY 5

Cultivate a resilient mindset that allows you to remain unaffected by the actions of others, whether positive or negative. Remember, you cannot control how people behave. Practice forgiveness regularly and let go of anger to maintain your inner peace.

How: Philippians 4:6–7; 2 Timothy 1:7; James 1:19–20

JULY 6

I'm fifty-six years old and just completed a 2.5-mile run. I started with a warm-up at a ten-minute mile pace, followed by two-minute intervals at a pace of 7:41 per mile. According to the first law of motion, an object in motion tends to stay in motion. Throughout life, there will be times when inactivity creeps in. However, if you can remain consistent with your physical activity, you'll spare yourself the struggle of getting back into shape. Remember, good health is the greatest wealth you can possess.

How: 1 Corinthians 6:19–20; Proverbs 3:7–8

_____

_____

_____

JULY 7

Learning a new language offers numerous advantages. It enhances your understanding of a culture, allowing for a deeper appreciation of its nuances. Additionally, it encourages you to focus more on listening to others when they speak in their native language, rather than just preparing your response.

How: James 1:19; 1 Corinthians 14:10

_____

_____

_____

JULY 8

Teasing often stems from those who perceive themselves as less successful than you. People who are more accomplished typically won't criticize or mock you; such behavior usually originates from individuals at a lower level of success.

How: Proverbs 26:18–19; Ephesians 4:29

_____

_____

_____

JULY 9

Cultivate your success quietly. Showcasing your accomplishments can inflate your ego. Additionally, publicizing your success may attract insincere friends and breed jealousy.

How: Ephesians 4:2; James 4:10; Micah 6:8

_____

_____

_____

JULY 10

If you feel the need to share information on social media, do so thoughtfully. Avoid inciting anger or spreading negativity. Approach your words and actions with humility and kindness.

How: Philippians 4:5; Galatians 5:22–23

JULY 11

One of life's greatest challenges is navigating setbacks. Without failures, there can be no growth or learning. You may be closer to a breakthrough than you think. Those with limited perspectives and weaker resolve tend to surrender quickly. Stay determined and keep moving forward.

How: Hebrews 12:1–2; James 1:12

JULY 12

Six months of dedication can yield remarkable results. Keep in mind that it takes just three weeks for an action to become a habit. Malcolm Gladwell suggests that achieving mastery requires around ten thousand hours of practice. Now, consider an endeavor that seems entirely impractical. If you commit two hours each day to pursuing your dream, it would take approximately 13.7 years to master it. By increasing your commitment to four hours a day, that timeline shortens to 6.8 years. Choose your path wisely.

How: Philippians 4:13; Job 5:17

JULY 13

Humor serves as an excellent coping mechanism for anxiety, helping to alleviate stress and facilitating an open mindset toward new possibilities. It's important, however, to ensure that your humor doesn't unintentionally harm others. Wise individuals can embrace self-deprecating humor without feeling ashamed.

How: Proverbs 17:22; Psalm 126:2; Ephesians 5:4

JULY 14

Continuously examine your conscience and unconscious biases. Bias operates as a quick-response mechanism within the lower brainstem, enabling rapid evaluations of situations. By engaging in self-reflection and fostering awareness, you can enhance your clarity of thought. This approach allows you to appreciate the beauty and potential inherent in our humanity.

How: 1 Peter 3:3–4; 2 Corinthians 4:16

JULY 15

A significant amount of energy is wasted when tasks are rushed. Instead, allocate focused and intentional time to enhance the learning process. Lackluster results often stem from mental fatigue.

How: Psalm 37:7; James 5:7–11

JULY 16

Everyone seems to be in a rush these days. We speed through our drives, munch our meals quickly, and skim through our reading. It feels as though people are racing toward an elusive sense of peace. But when was the last time you took a moment to sit in silence, free from time pressures, to converse and listen to God? True peace is found not in hurried efforts but in taking each step alongside Him—relying on His strength rather than your own.

How: Matthew 6:6; Mark 1:35

_____

_____

_____

JULY 17

Charity starts at home, and your friends can be considered part of your family. However, this doesn't imply that you should overlook those who are in need. Your family should always be your top priority.

How: Ephesians 6:1–4; 1 Timothy 5:8

_____

_____

_____

JULY 18

Once, a young student approached his teacher and asked, "Master, what is the secret to happiness?"

The teacher replied, "It's to avoid arguing with fools."

Perplexed, the student responded, "That can't be the secret!"

The teacher smiled and said, "You're right." And with that, the lesson concluded.

How: Proverbs 26:4–5; Proverbs 29:9; 2 Timothy 2:23

_____

_____

_____

JULY 19

Offer financial assistance to your friends without anticipating repayment. Your generosity reflects your affection for them. The joy derived from their companionship is invaluable.

How: Luke 10:25–37

_____

_____

_____

JULY 20

Exhibiting firmness can be a form of kindness in certain circumstances. It's essential to stay calm, well-prepared, and determined while in a leadership role. When faced with challenges, avoid giving in to emotions or reacting to insults, as these are tactics often used by those lacking understanding.

How: 1 Corinthians 16:13; 1 Timothy 4:12; Psalm 46:10

JULY 21

What if I told you that everyone has the potential to achieve par in golf, but practicing alone won't necessarily ensure a perfect round? The main reasons many golfers struggle are overestimating their skills (ego), taking unnecessary risks (planning), allowing emotions to interfere (focus), and making poor club choices (intelligence).

This concept is best illustrated by a story my dad shared with me. He was an accomplished golfer who earned a scholarship to Texas A&M. One day, he played a round with the eighty-year-old groundskeeper of the golf course. In his prime, my dad could drive the ball over 300 yards, while the groundskeeper could only manage about half that distance—yet he was straight and accurate. To everyone's surprise, the groundskeeper emerged victorious!

The groundskeeper had no ego. He played within his physical capabilities and possessed intimate knowledge of the course. Every shot he took was executed with the intention of preparing for the next one. In contrast, my dad, despite his impressive drives, often found himself in tougher positions with subsequent shots. Lacking familiarity with the course's finer details, he frequently had to react rather than plan ahead.

This lesson isn't confined to golf; it applies to life as well.

How: Proverbs 21:5; Proverbs 15:22

_____

_____

_____

JULY 22

A person without a goal is like a duck that cannot fly or swim. They tend to move aimlessly from one task to another, lacking focus and discipline. This approach makes life significantly more challenging and often results in feelings of apathy.

How: Proverbs 24:27; Proverbs 16:3

_____

_____

_____

JULY 23

Expressing complaints seldom improves a difficult situation; rather, it can intensify the burden. Instead, maintain a calm mindset and concentrate on what is within your control. You always have the power to choose how you respond to any circumstance.

How: Psalm 55:22; 1 Peter 5:7; Matthew 11:28–30

_____

_____

_____

JULY 24

Today, I celebrate my marriage to my wife, which began in 1999. I believe the key to a fulfilling marriage is prioritizing God first, your spouse second, and yourself last in all aspects of life.

How: 1 Corinthians 13:4–8

JULY 25

When Lamborghini was asked why they don't advertise on television, they explained that their target audience typically doesn't watch TV. The comforts of television can distract people from pursuing their dreams. If you took a week off to watch TV instead of investing that time in personal growth, would you come out ahead or behind?

How: Ephesians 5:16; 1 Corinthians 7:29–31

JULY 26

Your mind possesses the potential for boundless creativity. However, we often restrict ourselves by exerting too much pressure and succumbing to our biases. An open mind, free from the constraints of deadlines, can generate innovative solutions to our most significant challenges.

How: Romans 12:2; Exodus 35:31–32

JULY 27

In today's world, we are inundated with an overwhelming flow of information. It's essential to establish boundaries to safeguard your mental well-being. Much of this information is crafted to manipulate our primal instincts, which can drain our energy and diminish our cognitive functions.

How: Ecclesiastes 12:12; Proverbs 2:6

JULY 28

I liken life to running a mile on a track, consisting of four laps. During the first lap, you find that 80% of your competitors are still with you. By the second lap, that number dwindles to about 40%. This crucial lap highlights the extent of your preparation. The third lap, however, is the great equalizer, testing everyone's resilience. At this stage, it's a battle against the clock. While anyone can complete the final lap—even at a sprint—most often it's the fastest one, fueled by the anticipation of finishing the race. Embrace the challenges of the third lap. Overcome it through both mental fortitude and physical conditioning. This is the path to becoming a champion.

How: Romans 5:3–4; James 1:2–4

_____

_____

_____

JULY 29

We can learn about God through three interconnected approaches. The first is the call of the Holy Spirit. The second involves philosophical inquiry. The third is the study of theology. Always strive to deepen your relationship with God.

How: John 17:3; 2 Timothy 3:16; 1 John 4:1–3

_____

_____

_____

JULY 30

Refrain from alcohol! I'll emphasize this once more: avoid alcohol! It undermines your integrity, distances you from God, and can ultimately lead to financial ruin. It has been one of the most significant afflictions faced by humanity.

How: Ephesians 5:18; Galatians 5:21; 1 Corinthians 6:10

_____

_____

_____

JULY 31

Hard work fosters humility and gratitude. Avoid becoming too complacent by outsourcing every challenging task to contractors. Every type of work has its own inherent dignity.

How: Proverbs 14:23; Colossians 3:23; Ecclesiastes 9:10

_____

_____

_____

AUGUST 1

Speak only half as much as those around you. Embrace the power of silence. A person who talks excessively is like someone playing Texas Hold 'Em with their cards face up.

How: Proverbs 17:28; Proverbs 21:23

_____

_____

_____

AUGUST 2

There is a distinct difference between kindness and people-pleasing. Kindness is a genuine act of compassion directed toward another person, while people-pleasing is motivated by a desire for approval, often driven by the need to make others happy.

How: Galatians 1:10

_____

_____

_____

AUGUST 3

Keep your distance from people who are overly eager to please. They tend to mirror your personality and often lack their own opinions on important issues, aligning closely with yours. While they may boost your ego, their influence can ultimately lead to disappointment.

How: Proverbs 26:28; Psalm 12:2–3

AUGUST 4

In youth, there's often a strong desire to gain the approval of those around us, particularly parents, coaches, and teachers. While it's important to show respect to these figures, prioritizing their approval can hinder personal growth. In high school, I constantly sought to impress my track and field coach, which was easy due to my consistent victories in races. However, my true aspiration was to break the four-minute mile. My coach, focused on winning meets, would enter me in four different races at every competition, making it nearly impossible for me to achieve my goal. It's essential to cultivate the courage to respectfully express your own needs and boundaries.

How: Proverbs 3:6; Psalm 16:11

AUGUST 5

There is a wealth of beautiful prayers to discover, and I encourage you to explore as many as possible. Personally, one of my favorite approaches to prayer can be encapsulated by the acronym A.C.T.S:

- Adoration: Express your love for God.
- Confession: Acknowledge your shortcomings to Him.
- Thanksgiving: Share your gratitude for His blessings.
- Supplication: Present your needs and desires to God.

How: Philippians 4:6–7; Matthew 6:6–13; 1 Thessalonians 5:16–18

AUGUST 6

Farming offers numerous valuable lessons, particularly when examining grapes. The finest vintages around the globe often arise from measured stress brought on by weather conditions. In optimal weather, the vine channels its energy into producing more leaves. However, when faced with stress, the vine focuses its efforts on producing grapes, ensuring the seeds within can thrive and facilitate the next generation. This principle reflects a broader truth applicable to life itself.

How: Ecclesiastes 11:4–6; Matthew 13:3–8

_____

_____

_____

AUGUST 7

Familiarize yourself with the Saints in heaven. They act as intercessors, spiritual guides, and exemplars of a life devoted to God. Saint Padre Pio famously stated, "After my death, I will do even more. My true mission will commence after I pass away."

How: Revelation 8:3–4; Romans 1:7

_____

_____

_____

AUGUST 8

Life will inevitably present challenges. In the moment, these challenges can seem overwhelming. However, within twenty-four hours, their significance often diminishes by about half. Within a week, you'll find that they shrink even further, down by another 50%. A few months later, the issue will likely become a distant memory. It's wise to refrain from making decisions in the heat of the moment, unless the situation is truly critical.

How: James 1:12; Psalm 46:1; John 16:33

AUGUST 9

The pleasures of life are truly remarkable. God cares for us deeply and desires our happiness. Yet, the joys we find in this world are fleeting. I recall the excitement of buying my first sports car, luxury watch, or home. In those moments, I experienced immense joy, but that feeling faded over time. Conversely, what lasts through any decline in happiness is the impact we have on the lives of others.

How: Ecclesiastes 1:2; John 13:34–35; John 3:16

AUGUST 10

One of the most challenging aspects of life to master is the art of rest and recovery. Whether in sports, work, academics, or any creative endeavor, growth often occurs during periods of rest. This may seem counterintuitive—it's easy to believe that relentless effort is the key to success. However, neglecting rest can result in injuries and burnout. Therefore, it's essential to prioritize recovery and ensure adequate rest during any demanding activity.

How: Matthew 11:28; Hebrews 4:9–11; Genesis 2:2–3

AUGUST 11

Allow the Holy Spirit to guide you in all aspects of your life. This journey requires both faith and self-discipline. The most effective approach is to practice self-denial.

How: Acts 1:8; Romans 8:26

AUGUST 12

I adore this saying: People enter your life for a reason, a season, or a lifetime. Regardless of the duration of their presence, it's essential to treat everyone with compassion and kindness when they leave. These individuals are placed in your life by God to facilitate your growth and sanctification.

How: John 13:34; Leviticus 19:18; 1 Peter 2:17

AUGUST 13

Not every discussion needs your input; sometimes, silence is the wisest choice. You'll come across individuals who thrive on conflict and debate, often listening merely to prepare their next response rather than to understand. Avoid wasting your precious time and energy on such interactions.

How: Proverbs 26:20–21; 2 Timothy 2:23–26; Proverbs 15:18

AUGUST 14

Each morning, I like to offer this simple prayer: Lord Jesus Christ, please heal me, protect me, and surround me with Your divine love and grace today, so that Your will may be accomplished, not my own.

How: Psalm 59:16; Lamentations 3:22–23

AUGUST 15

I suggest giving CrossFit a try for a bit. It imparts several valuable life lessons. Despite being in a class with people of varying fitness levels, your only competition is yourself. Each workout is meant to challenge you, and you must learn to keep pushing forward. Over time, developing strength and flexibility yields the most significant advantages.

How: 1 Timothy 4:8; Romans 12:1

AUGUST 16

Honor the patriots who gave everything to ensure the continuation of the great American experiment. I once spoke with an Airborne Army Captain who lost his leg in the Iraq War, asking him how I could best honor veterans. He replied, "Make your life worthy of their sacrifice." This wise counsel has stayed with me ever since.

How: Romans 12:10; 1 Peter 2:17; Ephesians 4:32

AUGUST 17

Here is a lesson I learned from doing a very difficult CrossFit workout today:

It's incredible how we can psych ourselves out before a workout even begins. When I first saw the difficult routine, my initial thought was that I would never be able to complete it! Observing the class before me only reinforced my doubts—everyone looked like they were struggling. Running used to be my strength, but I noticed the intensity was brutal this time. My coach decided to scale back my cleans from 95 lbs. to 45 lbs., and I'm so grateful for that thoughtful coaching. Yes, I'm sore now, and I know I will feel even more sore tomorrow. However, this workout allowed me to reflect on a broader life lesson: don't let self-doubt take over before you even start the hard work. Challenges will arise, and they might feel tough and intense, but remember to catch your breath and stay hydrated. The key is to keep pushing forward and not give up. Now it's time to enjoy a hearty protein breakfast! Best of all, I made it through!

Workout: Hot Shots 19
6 Rounds for Time
- 30 Air squats
- 19 Power cleans (135/95 lbs.)
- 7 Strict pull-ups
- 400-meter run
Time Cap = 45:00

How: Philippians 4:13; 1 Peter 5:7; Matthew 6:34

_____

_____

_____

AUGUST 18

What fascinates me is that a human can create Liszt's Mephisto Waltz No. 1. Moreover, a person can breathe life into this music by playing it flawlessly from memory. In each phrase, the pianist infuses their own unique passion into the performance, making it truly distinctive. It's evident that there is something profoundly divine at work in this process.

How: Matthew 19:26; Luke 18:27

_____

_____

_____

AUGUST 19

I stand in support of this remarkable American experiment. I honor our troops who dedicate themselves to serving our country, as well as the first responders bravely working under challenging conditions today. I uphold the fundamental American values of life, liberty, and the pursuit of happiness. I believe in our right to protest freely and cherish our Constitution. I defend our God-given right to protect our freedoms through the Second Amendment. In this great nation, you have the freedom to worship without fear of persecution. You reside in the most prosperous country in the world. I trust in our elected leaders to represent and serve the interests of the people. In this land of opportunity, you can become whatever you aspire to be. I value diversity and respect differing viewpoints. This is what makes me proud to be an American.

How: Proverbs 14:34; Jeremiah 29:7; Romans 13:1–7

AUGUST 20

Discover how to create a remarkable dish that can become your signature recipe to impress anyone. Prepare it frequently for friends, a potential partner, or even a new acquaintance. This simple gesture expresses immense gratitude and care toward others.

How: 1 Peter 4:9; Hebrews 13:2

_____

_____

_____

AUGUST 21

A friend of mine once shared a thought-provoking story about the concept of value. Consider a bottle of water: at a discount store, you might find one for about $0.99. In a party store, it could cost around $2.00, and at an airport, it might be priced at $5.00. Its perceived worth fluctuates based on the context in which it is sold. While you are not a bottle of water, the lesson is clear: don't accept an environment that fails to recognize your true worth.

How: Ephesians 2:10; Genesis 1:26–27; Isaiah 43:4

_____

_____

_____

AUGUST 22

During my youth, I dedicated a significant amount of time to the outdoors. The skills gained from camping and immersing oneself in nature are truly priceless. They foster creativity and teach adaptability in the face of challenges. In today's digital age, many individuals may find themselves at a loss if that virtual realm were to disappear. It's essential to stay prepared.

How: 1 Peter 3:15; Proverbs 6:6–8

_____

_____

_____

AUGUST 23

The impact of our spoken words and thoughts is immense. Always refrain from expressing negativity about yourself or others. Your spoken words can unconsciously shape your thoughts. Remember to practice kindness toward yourself.

How: Colossians 3:12; 1 Corinthians 9:25–27

_____

_____

_____

AUGUST 24

There will be days when you wake up feeling as if you're not making any headway toward your dreams. Embrace those days! Consider them as a test of your determination. Many people choose to give up when encountering challenges, often unaware of how close they are to a breakthrough. I'm reminded of Mike Tyson's famous quote: "Everyone has a plan until they get punched in the face." While pursuing your dreams, expect to get hit—sometimes more than once. Learn to roll with the punches and refuse to let them bring you down. You are more resilient than you realize.

How: Romans 5:3–5; James 1:2–4; Isaiah 41:10

_____

_____

_____

AUGUST 25

I may not be a theologian, but it's clear that when Jesus instructs us to follow Him, it's not just a solitary pursuit. In the Gospels of Luke and Matthew, He emphasizes the importance of taking up our cross daily. Historical estimates suggest that Jesus' cross weighed around 300 pounds, and after enduring severe beatings for our sins, He carried it for approximately 2,000 feet. While this journey will undoubtedly be challenging, remember that you are never alone; Jesus will always be there to support you!

How: Matthew 16:24–26; Luke 9:23; Matthew 28:20

_____

_____

_____

AUGUST 26

God is constantly working on your growth and sanctification, offering beautiful lessons at just the right moments. One such lesson unfolded when my wife lost her vision. I had to learn to see the world through her eyes, which was both daunting and disheartening. It wasn't solely about performing tasks for her that she could no longer manage; it was fundamentally about connecting with her through empathy. It was about helping her preserve her dignity and anticipating challenges from her perspective, all while feeling guided by God. Now, imagine applying this insight to every aspect of your life.

How: Galatians 5:13–14; Isaiah 58:10; Philippians 1:6

_____

_____

_____

AUGUST 27

I'd like to share how I came to embrace Catholicism. I was baptized and confirmed in the Episcopal Church, where I served as a dedicated acolyte for many years. Both of my parents were also Episcopalian, which fostered my deep affection for the Episcopal tradition.

During my mother's health decline while in hospice care, I noticed that a Catholic priest was the only religious figure visiting her. This experience profoundly impacted me. I also found great solace in praying at a Catholic church during that difficult time. Driven by a desire to deepen my understanding, I dedicated myself to exploring the Catholic faith. This journey involved extensive reading, witnessing miracles firsthand, completing the RCIA program, and engaging in discussions with theologians.

I believe that the Holy Spirit guided me to the Catholic Church, drawing me closer to Jesus. I encourage you to delve into Christian theology as well—there's much to learn and discover.

How: 1 John 5:20; 2 Peter 3:18; 1 John 2:3–5

_____

_____

_____

AUGUST 28

I have a deep conviction in the real presence of Jesus in the Catholic Eucharist. Numerous miracles have been attributed to the Eucharist, and there is a wealth of literature and evidence supporting these occurrences. Personally, I witnessed the Holy Blood of Jesus on the Corporal in Orvieto, Italy, which brings me immense joy.

How: John 6:54–57; Matthew 26:26–29; 1 Corinthians 10:16

AUGUST 29

When investigating an organization or opportunity, I find that engaging in simple conversations is the most effective way to understand the environment. Once trust is built, individuals are more likely to share insights that aren't immediately visible. It's essential to hone this skill. In today's landscape, where marketing is pervasive, it's crucial to delve deeper to uncover the truth.

How: James 1:5–6; 1 Thessalonians 5:21

AUGUST 30

As I write this, Artificial Intelligence (AI) is beginning to thrive globally, presenting numerous possibilities, both beneficial and detrimental. It is essential to recognize the distinction between what is created by human hands and what is divine. God has fashioned us in His image, and nothing devised by humans or machines can ever exceed the love that God has for us. Our humanity is both unique and sacred.

How: Genesis 11:1–9; Psalm 8:4–6

_____

_____

_____

AUGUST 31

I've experienced both physical health and illness throughout my life, and I believe that diet plays a crucial role in determining our well-being. Monitoring your nutrition and macronutrients empowers you to make more informed food choices. Additionally, pre-planning your meals for the day can help you resist the temptation of impulsive decisions that often result in fast food.

How: Proverbs 23:20–21; 1 Corinthians 6:19–20

_____

_____

_____

SEPTEMBER 1

One day, you will find yourself in a leadership role. Keep in mind Machiavelli's insightful words: "There is nothing so challenging to manage, so uncertain of success, or so unpredictable as leading people." This quote highlights one of the key reasons why achieving excellence can be so challenging.

How: Matthew 20:25–28; Titus 1:6–9

SEPTEMBER 2

Living a healthy life demands discipline. It's essential to actively oversee what you allow into your body—not just in terms of nutrition, but also regarding information, negativity, positive emotions, your environment, and all forms of stimulation. Understand the cause and effect of these factors and make informed choices.

How: Philippians 4:8

SEPTEMBER 3

In this life, suffering is an inevitable part of the human experience. I encourage you to embrace redemptive suffering during these challenging times. Consider offering your own struggles to God as a prayer for someone else. There is no stronger connection to the Cross of Jesus than when we unite our suffering with His for the sake of another soul. Remember, Christ is present with you in these moments of pain and hardship.

How: Romans 5:3–5; John 16:33; 1 Peter 4:12–13

_____

_____

_____

SEPTEMBER 4

You will encounter injustice and behavior that goes against the teachings of the Gospel throughout life. We are called to detest the sin while still loving the sinner. Jesus exemplified this profound truth on the cross when He declared, "Father, forgive them, for they do not know what they are doing." Let your actions clearly reflect your identity as a Christian. Continuously pray for the transformation of those who stray from the path. Approach them with a compassionate heart.

How: Romans 5:8; John 3:16; Luke 23:34

_____

_____

_____

SEPTEMBER 5

A Prayer Before Enduring Suffering.

Dear and compassionate God,

I humbly offer my suffering for this specific intention. May it be laid at the foot of Jesus' cross, and may it be pleasing in every way as I seek to unite myself with my Savior, Jesus Christ. All praise, honor, and glory belong to You forever. Amen.

Through this prayer, may I find the strength to confront any physical or mental struggle that lies ahead.

How: Philippians 4:13

_____

_____

_____

SEPTEMBER 6

Develop a routine of monitoring several important health metrics regularly. This includes tracking your weight, blood pressure, resting heart rate, and blood sugar levels. Ensure you undergo a comprehensive blood panel test annually. Schedule a yearly appointment with your doctor and visit your dentist every six months. Treat your body with the dedication it deserves, as if you were destined to live for a millennium. Nurture your soul with the urgency as if each day could be your last.

How: 1 Corinthians 6:19–20; Proverbs 17:22; John 10:10

_____

_____

_____

SEPTEMBER 7

A storm can be seen from various perspectives. When you're in the sunlight and see a storm approaching, it appears particularly ominous. Inside the storm, you can feel the wind and rain, but it doesn't seem as dark as it does from outside. Once the storm has passed, a sense of calm and a refreshing quality envelops the air. Things are rarely as bleak as they appear, and, like everything in life, this too shall pass.

How: Psalm 107:29; Isaiah 43:2; Deuteronomy 31:6

_____

_____

_____

SEPTEMBER 8

Trust is fundamental in all areas of life. It serves as the cornerstone for friendships, business relationships, marriages, and effective leadership. This precious bond should always be respected and protected. Once established, it opens the door to limitless possibilities. However, trust must be cultivated and reaffirmed on a daily basis.

How: Psalm 145:13; Proverbs 12:22

SEPTEMBER 9

Prioritize embarking on a faith-based pilgrimage. My experience in Italy was transformative; I witnessed a daily miracle. The blessings you encounter will stay with you for a lifetime.

How: 2 Corinthians 5:7; Psalm 119:105

SEPTEMBER 10

I met a remarkable individual who grew up by the ocean in Western Canada. He shared a story from his childhood, reflecting on his experience of growing up in poverty. Every day, his father would fish to support the family, often bringing home salmon, Dungeness crab, and halibut. One day, overwhelmed by his circumstances, he asked his father, "Why can't we have hot dogs like the rich kids?" It's a poignant reminder of how easily we can overlook our own blessings.

How: Colossians 3:17; 1 Thessalonians 5:16–18

_____

_____

_____

SEPTEMBER 11

On this day in 2001, I was on a flight when the attacks on the World Trade Center occurred. I frequently took similar flights and had spent considerable time at the World Trade Center itself. I safely landed in Chicago as events unfolded dramatically around me. If you ever find yourself in a comparable situation, conquer your fears, stay composed, concentrate on what you can control, assist those around you, and have a plan in place to safeguard your loved ones. Make it a priority to communicate with them swiftly and often, if possible.

How: Psalm 91:1–6; Joshua 1:9; Psalm 56:3–4

SEPTEMBER 12

I hold a firm stance on alcohol consumption: if you don't drink, it's best not to start. Alcohol is a toxin that can lead to weight gain, increased vulnerability to illness, and impaired cognitive function. When faced with situations where alcohol is being offered, opt for a seltzer water with a lime instead; it will appear as though you are enjoying a drink without consuming alcohol. Additionally, avoid being in settings where you might be photographed around alcohol or individuals who are intoxicated.

How: Ephesians 5:18; Proverbs 23:20–21

SEPTEMBER 13

Yesterday, I overheard someone calling their father dumb. It's important to remember to never disrespect your parents or anyone else for that matter. You should always aim to honor your parents, as the sacrifices they make for your well-being often go unrecognized until you experience adulthood yourself.

How: Exodus 20:12; Ephesians 6:1–3

SEPTEMBER 14

One of my favorite quotes that reminds me to stay humble comes from one of the wisest individuals in history, Socrates: "I know that I know nothing." Those who boast about their intelligence only reveal their foolishness. Moreover, an arrogant demeanor can push people away and erode trust. Wisdom, knowledge, and understanding are blessings bestowed by the Holy Spirit, and not everyone possesses these gifts. It's important to approach them with humility, gratitude, and respect.

How: Proverbs 16:18; Proverbs 16:19; 1 Corinthians 12:8

SEPTEMBER 15

When I greet people in the morning, I often say, "God has created another beautiful day!" Whether it's raining or sunny, the perfection of His creations remains unchanged. Shifting our focus to His works fosters a sense of piety, gratitude, and humility. Each day presents incredible opportunities to love and serve Him.

How: Psalm 100:2; Colossians 3:23; Romans 12:11

SEPTEMBER 16

I previously spoke to you about the importance of offering your suffering to God as a means of redemption. In addition, it's essential to cultivate the habit of presenting our blessings to Him as well. When we experience joy and receive wonderful things, we often overlook their true source—our Savior, Jesus Christ. By adopting this perspective, you will find yourself consistently offering everything to God, and the graces that flow back to you will far surpass all the stars in the sky.

How: Psalm 107:1; Colossians 3:17; Philippians 4:6

SEPTEMBER 17

Opera is a form of art that often needs time to be appreciated fully. My high school music teacher first exposed me to this captivating genre, and my experience watching *The Magic Flute* by Wolfgang Amadeus Mozart left a lasting impression on me. It's remarkable to consider that such extraordinary beauty was crafted without any digital assistance. Supporting this art form, which deeply resonates with our shared humanity, is essential. Let us be generous in our contributions to the arts, particularly opera.

How: Colossians 3:23; Psalm 59:16

SEPTEMBER 18

When embarking on the journey of learning something new, it's essential to set aside your ego. Don't feel embarrassed or intimidated by your lack of understanding. Avoid comparing your learning style to that of others; instead, embrace curiosity and ask plenty of questions. At times, stepping away from a problem can be beneficial if you find yourself struggling. Remember, even the greatest thinkers throughout history have faced similar challenges.

How: Proverbs 1:5; Proverbs 1:7; Proverbs 9:9

SEPTEMBER 19

Throughout your life, you will encounter numerous opportunities to give presentations. The cornerstone of an effective presentation lies in compelling storytelling and thorough preparation. Our brains are structured to process information sequentially. The primitive brain stem governs our fight-or-flight responses, followed by the limbic system, which is responsible for storing emotions. Finally, the cerebral cortex manages our higher cognitive functions. To engage the higher levels of processing, you must first connect with the lower brain. Storytelling serves to calm the audience, evoke emotions, and facilitate deeper learning and reflection.

How: Ephesians 4:29; Colossians 4:6; Proverbs 18:21

_____

_____

_____

SEPTEMBER 20

Living a virtuous life can often feel isolating. It's that sense of loneliness when those around you are celebrating while you head home to focus on your studies or work. You may feel as if everyone else is enjoying life more than you are. In those moments, turn your heart toward God. Resist the urge to succumb to regret, depression, or anxiety. Remember, you are never truly alone on this journey. The Holy Spirit resides within you, guiding your every step. The true reward of a virtuous life is virtue itself. In contrast, those who live impulsively for the moment are on a troubling path toward destruction.

How: 2 Peter 1:5–7; Philippians 4:8

_____

_____

_____

SEPTEMBER 21

Not all of your actions need to be publicized. Sometimes, it's better to allow the most compassionate and humble deeds to remain unseen, known only to God. Keep in mind that your efforts should reflect the influence of the Holy Spirit rather than come from your own desires.

How: Matthew 6:6; 1; 1 Thessalonians 4:11

_____

_____

_____

SEPTEMBER 22

The greatest gift you can offer someone is your complete attention. This gesture is genuinely palpable. Every musician who has performed live will attest to sensing the audience's energy. When listeners focus their attention on the performer, magical music unfolds.

How: James 1:19; Proverbs 18:13

_____

_____

_____

SEPTEMBER 23

You will come across many homeless individuals in this world. It's important not to overlook them. If you have the means, consider offering them assistance. Even more impactful is taking the time to engage in conversation and share a kind word. Providing a nourishing meal can make a significant difference. We all face challenges in life, and some may have fallen and just need a helping hand to rise again.

How: Matthew 25:44

_____

_____

_____

SEPTEMBER 24

Some days, you might wake up without a sense of joy and even feel a little down. During those times, taking a walk—preferably in nature—can be beneficial. It's essential to listen to your body when it signals the need for rest and healing. Remember, when you have entrusted your life to Jesus Christ, the light of joy within you can never truly be extinguished.

How: Philippians 4:4; Galatians 5:22–23; Romans 15:13

SEPTEMBER 25

You will encounter numerous opportunities to address groups, whether it's a small gathering or a large audience. Before you begin speaking, take a moment to pray to the Holy Spirit. Ask for humility and submit yourself to His guidance. Remember, God deserves all the honor, glory, and power in everything we undertake.

How: Romans 8:26–27; Jude 1:20

SEPTEMBER 26

"Trust your instruments" is a vital mantra in aviation. In situations of low visibility, spatial disorientation, or overwhelming physical sensations, relying on your instruments can be a matter of life or death. This principle extends beyond aviation and into our everyday lives. Place your trust in Jesus first, and let your values, firmly rooted in the Gospel, guide you. By doing so, you will be able to withstand any storm that comes your way.

How: Proverbs 3:5–6; Psalm 28:7; Jeremiah 17:7

SEPTEMBER 27

I receive numerous messages on LinkedIn from individuals who send me unsolicited pitches about how they can assist my business, often without any understanding of me, my company, or the industry we're in. It's akin to shouting into the wind during rush hour in a New York subway. However, there's an important lesson here: if you're not willing to take the time to understand my business before presenting an idea, how can I trust you with my data?

How: Ephesians 4:2–3; Proverbs 1:5; Proverbs 18:15

SEPTEMBER 28

Today, I fondly recall the day I met my future wife back in 1990 during a class at The University of Michigan. Her beauty was truly captivating. I gathered the courage to invite her for coffee after class, and to my delight, she accepted. You never know when you might encounter the person you're destined to be with. It's essential to approach new connections with an open heart, kindness, and compassion. Our relationship would never have blossomed if I hadn't taken that first step with warmth and sincerity.

How: Proverbs 18:22; 2 Corinthians 6:14

SEPTEMBER 29

I listened to an interview with Elvis Presley, and when asked if he had written any of his songs, he responded, "I wish I could; I was fortunate to graduate from high school." Despite his immense fame and wealth, there was a palpable sadness in his inability to create music. This reflects how we often struggle in silence over what we lack, overshadowing the joys we do have.

How: Ecclesiastes 5:18–19

SEPTEMBER 30

When providing criticism, try to present two or three constructive suggestions for improvement. This approach shows that you're more focused on solutions rather than merely pointing out flaws. By offering helpful ideas that alleviate the challenges faced by the individual, you can foster a lasting friendship. However, if your suggestions are not accepted, recognize that the issue may have its own purpose, and it might be best to step back from the situation.

How: Romans 8:28; 2 Corinthians 4:16–18

_____

_____

_____

OCTOBER 1

A career typically unfolds in three distinct stages: the learning phase, the earning phase, and the giving phase. Earning is a reflection of the learning that has taken place, while learning is often the result of giving. The true fulfillment comes from the giving stage. While many tend to focus on giving back later in their careers, consider the impact you could have if you prioritized giving from the very beginning.

How: Matthew 6:1–4; Proverbs 11:24–25; Proverbs 22:9

_____

_____

_____

OCTOBER 2

Become someone who embraces the small actions that transform a situation into a memorable experience. Undertake these gestures quietly, without seeking recognition. There are always chances to enhance the moment. The true reward lies in enriching the experience for others. Additionally, you cultivate a mindset grounded in servant leadership.

How: Matthew 22:39; John 13:14–17

OCTOBER 3

To my dear goddaughters,

As you navigate through life, remember that the right man will truly appreciate your worth. Choosing a spouse who aligns with God's plan for you requires both patience and discernment. Pay close attention to their values; ensure that their actions reflect their words. Always prioritize principles over passion. Allow your partner to demonstrate their love for you wholeheartedly— through their heart, mind, and soul. You are deserving of love and respect, so never lose sight of this truth.

How: Psalm 37:4; Genesis 2:24; Ephesians 5:25

OCTOBER 4

There are numerous religions in the world that differ from Christianity, yet there is only one true path to heaven through Jesus Christ. Throughout history, world wars have erupted due to religious differences. As believers, we are called to spread the Gospel of Jesus Christ, a significant and profound responsibility. Fortunately, we have the guidance of the Holy Spirit to support us on this journey.

It's essential to approach others' beliefs with sensitivity, avoiding any actions that might cause harm or embarrassment. We should embody the Gospel through our actions, demonstrating compassion and love. For those who do not have Jesus Christ as their Savior, life can be filled with many challenges and struggles. Therefore, let us always strive to draw people closer to Jesus.

How: John 14:6; Matthew 28:19–20; Mark 16:15–16; Ephesians 4:32

OCTOBER 5

Life is a valuable gift from God, deserving of protection at all costs. This encompasses both the unborn and the elderly. It involves the daily decisions we make to ensure our communities support their most vulnerable members. Additionally, it reflects our personal choices regarding self-care. You were not created by chance; God designed you for a unique and purposeful role.

How: Psalm 139:13–16; Matthew 6:26; Luke 1:44; Jeremiah 1:5

OCTOBER 6

You can provide your wise counsel to individuals or groups, but how they receive it is not your responsibility. This can be particularly challenging when it comes to family and close friends. Before sharing your advice with others, consider presenting it to Jesus, and do so with love and compassion. Remember, God continuously invites us to experience His boundless mercy and love.

How: Proverbs 19:17; Galatians 6:10

OCTOBER 7

Materialism can be a perilous obsession that distances individuals from God's love. In youth, it's easy to elevate possessions, thinking true happiness is found in them. However, after obtaining these items, their appeal often diminishes rapidly. Even the most cherished treasures will eventually lose their shine. In contrast, God's love for us remains unwavering. Make your choices thoughtfully.

How: Hebrews 13:5; Luke 12:15

OCTOBER 8

There's a profound saying that has shaped my approach to personal relationships: "Comparison is the thief of joy." Throughout life, you'll meet individuals who may feel jealous of you, a response rooted in primitive instincts. Since you cannot control how others respond to you, I suggest practicing humility in every situation. True strength lies in humility. Jealousy, much like materialism, often stems from the belief that happiness exists in someone else's life rather than in one's own. Remember, you are made perfectly by God, who desires for you to experience genuine joy as His creation.

How: Proverbs 14:30; Proverbs 27:4; James 3:16

OCTOBER 9

There are occasions when a situation demands a prompt response and action. However, this is not usually the case. Unless it is genuinely a matter of life and death, taking a moment to gather your thoughts is often the wisest approach. When your emotional state has a chance to settle, you are more likely to discover solutions that benefit everyone involved. A sense of urgency can give rise to various unintended emotions, such as anxiety, envy, anger, and depression, among others.

How: Proverbs 27:1; Philippians 4:6–7; 1 Peter 5:7

OCTOBER 10

There is a feeling more painful than simply failing to finish a race: it's crossing the finish line with the knowledge that you could have performed better. I hope you never have to endure that sensation. These unfortunate individuals never experience the thrill of victory or the sting of defeat; instead, they find solace in comfort, which gradually drags them into an abyss from which there is no escape, ultimately leading to their demise. The race is life!

How: Ecclesiastes 9:10; Galatians 6:9

OCTOBER 11

Life is about the journey, not just the destination. Joy, success, and fulfillment are not simply waiting for you at the end; they are accessible to you in the present moment. Don't rush ahead so quickly that you overlook the blessings that surround you each day. Every heartbeat is a treasured gift from God.

How: Ecclesiastes 2:24–26; Psalm 16:11; Romans 15:13

OCTOBER 12

Steer clear of confrontations whenever possible. It's important to know when to disengage from a situation that could escalate into physical violence. However, this doesn't mean you shouldn't be equipped to defend yourself. Consider taking classes in karate or boxing to master self-defense techniques. Your goal should be to neutralize a threat swiftly and safely. If a fight becomes unavoidable, confront it with the determination of a lion, ensuring that your assailant is rendered unable to cause harm again.

How: Ephesians 6:12; Exodus 14:14; Psalm 144:1

OCTOBER 13

Exercise caution when meeting new people. While it's important to extend kindness and compassion to everyone, it's equally essential to quickly understand their values. Additionally, avoid surrounding yourself with individuals who are unaware of their own limitations, as they may unintentionally lead you into risky situations.

How: Proverbs 14:16–18; Proverbs 14:7–9

_____

_____

_____

OCTOBER 14

Today, I encountered a special moment during breakfast with my friends in East Lansing. An elderly gentleman named Nick joined us at our table after following my friend into the restaurant, settling in as if we were long-lost friends. Within a couple of minutes, it became evident that he was experiencing dementia. He ordered breakfast with us, and we kindly decided to cover his meal. Throughout our time together, he shared several unusual stories, and we made an effort to remain engaged and compassionate. Afterward, I spoke with the waitress to see if Nick needed any assistance. She smiled and informed me that he was a regular and that our kindness truly brightened his day.

How: Colossians 3:12; Proverbs 21:21; 1 Corinthians 13:4

OCTOBER 15

To truly understand a city and its inhabitants, explore its parks. A remarkable city takes pride in maintaining its parks in excellent condition. If you notice residents frequently enjoying these spaces, it's a good indicator of a compassionate and inclusive culture. Keep this in mind when choosing a place to call home; you'll want to avoid cities where the parks are neglected.

How: Ecclesiastes 2:5; Jeremiah 29:5

OCTOBER 16

Much like my previous message about parks, if you want to gain insight into an organization or business, take a look at its common areas. Places like the café, waiting rooms, and restrooms are excellent starting points. In my experience, organizations that strive for excellence never neglect their facilities. Excellence is a fundamental principle that permeates all aspects of an organization's operations. When one area is poorly maintained, it's likely that other areas will reflect the same lack of care.

How: Colossians 3:23–24; 1 Corinthians 10:31

OCTOBER 17

Whenever you begin to feel confident in your many talents, find a way to humble yourself. Ego can hinder personal growth and learning. Einstein mathematically described ego as the inverse of knowledge. The more humble you remain, the more you will observe and comprehend.

How: Proverbs 2:6; Proverbs 18:15; James 1:5

_____

_____

_____

OCTOBER 18

When someone hurts you, choose to rise above the situation. Resist the urge to respond with anger or seek revenge. Instead, cultivate a spirit of forgiveness. Often, the negative actions of others stem from their own deficiencies. Avoid matching insults with insults; instead, respond with kindness and love. Your opponent will likely be taken aback by your reaction.

How: Matthew 5:39; Luke 6:29

_____

_____

_____

OCTOBER 19

The Beatles, my favorite band, recorded a total of 213 songs during their peak popularity. Remarkably, the word "love" appears around 500 times throughout these tracks. This is not random; it reflects a universal desire for beauty. After all, love is often regarded as the most exquisite of all emotions.

How: John 13:34

_____

_____

_____

OCTOBER 20

Cultivating a daily practice of reading, writing, and praying can be transformative. These activities often serve as powerful healing tools that we tend to overlook. Reading fosters wisdom, writing enhances our communication skills, and prayer connects us deeply to our loving God in heaven.

How: 1 Thessalonians 5:17; Philippians 4:6–7; Joshua 1:8

_____

_____

_____

OCTOBER 21

Our actions should be thoroughly examined before we proceed with them. Even with the best intentions, we can inadvertently cause harm, and this process can help cultivate empathy. For instance, I once offered to give my sister-in-law a ride in her father's beloved sports car. I viewed it as a simple act of kindness that I thought would be appreciated. However, I didn't realize that it was the first time she had been in the car since her father's passing, and she had only ever ridden in it with him. This brought up a wave of sadness for her. Had I taken the time to ask questions before extending my offer, I might have recognized the emotional weight of the situation.

How: Romans 12:15; Ephesians 4:32; Hebrews 4:15

_____

_____

_____

OCTOBER 22

Wisdom surrounds us if we're willing to pay attention. In 2007, at L'Enfant Plaza subway station in Washington, D.C., renowned violinist Joshua Bell performed on his priceless Stradivarius for commuters. He started with Bach's Chaconne (Violin Partita No. 2 in D Minor), widely regarded as the pinnacle of solo violin compositions. Despite the hundreds who passed by, only a few paused to listen, and only one person recognized him. Don't rush through life, focused solely on reaching your next destination. Take a moment to stop and truly listen.

How: Ecclesiastes 3:1; Proverbs 19:2

_____

_____

_____

OCTOBER 23

Throughout life, you'll encounter numerous renowned individuals. Engaging in conversations with accomplished people across various fields can be thrilling. My experiences have taught me just how much we share in common. Often, we elevate famous figures to a pedestal, but there's no reason to feel intimidated. Instead, approach them with genuine kindness and authenticity. After all, we all originate from the same source.

How: 1 Peter 4:9; Romans 12:13

_____

_____

_____

OCTOBER 24

Liberal ideology is often mischaracterized as compassion, but many argue it can reflect intolerance. When engaging with someone who holds liberal views, be mindful of potential tactics such as gaslighting, name-calling, or hate speech. Remember that truth welcomes scrutiny, while falsehoods resist it. Approach conversations with kindness and empathy, but remain steadfast in your values. Aim to ask thoughtful questions that promote understanding rather than put the other person on the defensive.

How: Proverbs 4:7; Proverbs 18:2; Proverbs 14:29

OCTOBER 25

Study history to draw important lessons from it. Avoid repeating the mistakes of the past. Time does not improve a failed ideology, such as communism. It is vital to challenge and confront communist principles. Remaining silent is a disservice to the memory of the one hundred million individuals who lost their lives due to communist oppression. Be prepared to defend freedom, even at the cost of your own life if necessary.

How: Joshua 1:9; Deuteronomy 31:6

OCTOBER 26

There's a popular saying: "Do what makes you happy." I beg to differ. Instead, seek what makes you holy. Happiness is temporary, while holiness endures.

How: 1 Peter 1:15–16; Hebrews 12:14; Romans 6:22

OCTOBER 27

One of life's profound mysteries is the widespread belief in God, yet many individuals fail to act in accordance with His teachings. If you hold faith in an all-powerful, loving, and merciful God, what reason could there be for not following His guidance in all aspects of your life? True obedience demands wisdom, faith, and courage. Be ready to face societal challenges when you define what is considered right by human standards as wrong in the eyes of God.

How: 1 John 5:3; Isaiah 1:19; Acts 5:29

OCTOBER 28

Be mindful of the company you choose to keep. Ensure that your voice is distinctly yours, not a reflection of someone else's. One of the most remarkable songs ever written is "If I Can Dream," penned by Walter Earl Brown and famously performed by Elvis Presley. This song served as a tribute to Martin Luther King, Jr. and Robert F. Kennedy, both of whom were tragically assassinated in 1968. Initially, Elvis' manager, Colonel Tom Parker, opposed including this song in Elvis' TV Comeback Special. However, Elvis was determined and ultimately prevailed. It's said that his heartfelt performance moved the backup singer to tears.

When faced with strong-willed individuals who pressure you to act against your own desires, take the time to examine your own intentions to ensure they are sincere. Avoid getting bogged down in trying to decipher someone else's motives. Instead, have the courage to let your voice be heard.

How: Joshua 1:9; Philippians 4:8

_____

_____

_____

OCTOBER 29

Alter your environment to adjust your output. When you find your creativity waning, it's advisable not to force it. Instead, take a step back to gain perspective. Ludwig van Beethoven, for instance, found inspiration in his daily walks. There's a tale of him wandering through a park for hours, mentally composing despite being caught in a heavy downpour.

How: Ephesians 2:10; Proverbs 2

_____

_____

_____

OCTOBER 30

The world is home to a multitude of religions, with estimates suggesting there are around ten thousand. There is only one path to heaven, which is through Jesus Christ, our Savior. It can be tempting to criticize those who follow different faiths or do not believe in Jesus. It's crucial, though, not to serve as a stumbling block for others when it comes to accepting Jesus. This principle applies not only to what you say but also to how you behave. Embrace a respectful and nonjudgmental approach toward individuals of different beliefs, emphasizing our shared human aspirations and the elements of truth, while firmly holding onto the conviction that the fullness of truth and salvation is found in Jesus Christ.

How: Romans 14; John 3:16

_____

_____

_____

OCTOBER 31

You are more than just the sum of your strengths and weaknesses. Life isn't simply about achieving balance; it's about personal growth. A vital element of a fulfilling life is forgiveness. In the Lord's Prayer, we seek forgiveness not only for our own missteps but also for others. Be kind to yourself during your weak moments, and never lose the courage to rise again after a stumble. Remember, you are not alone in this journey.

How: John 21:15–17

NOVEMBER 1

Today marks All Saints' Day, a celebration that often goes unnoticed as Halloween steals the spotlight. It's important to observe this day with reverence. Take the time to attend Mass and pray for the saints. We are all called to pursue holiness and strive to become saints ourselves. Delve into the lives of the saints; they offer us valuable guidance on how to live.

How: Revelation 7:9–10; Wisdom of Solomon 3:1–9

NOVEMBER 2

Don't waste time! It's the most valuable resource you have, so give it your full attention. Always enter a meeting with a clear objective in mind. Minimize casual conversations during these meetings to stay focused. Aim to be a doer rather than just a talker. At the end of each day, reflect on how you spent your time and energy. Strive to improve by 1% each day.

How: Psalm 90:12; Ephesians 5:15–16

NOVEMBER 3

Give God the glory and honor for your achievements privately in your heart. Many may not celebrate your success due to jealousy. People often struggle to accept others who strive to improve themselves, especially if they are not willing or able to make those same sacrifices. Remember, you cannot control others' actions; you can only manage your own responses.

How: Proverbs 14:30; James 3:14–16; Proverbs 27:4; Galatians 5:19–21

NOVEMBER 4

It's often more effective to sever ties suddenly—be it in a personal or a business context—when you discover unethical behavior. As the Japanese proverb goes, "If you get on the wrong train, get off at the next station." The longer you remain on that train, the harder and more expensive it becomes to switch to the right one. There's no need to provide explanations or justifications; just end the relationship professionally. Often, those engaging in unethical conduct are unlikely to accept any rationale you provide. However, always offer forgiveness to them for their errors.

How: Psalm 1:1; 1 Peter 2:12; Proverbs 13:20; 2 Corinthians 6:14

NOVEMBER 5

Decision-making within organizations can be compared to a series of escalating challenges. At the operational level, issues arise every ten minutes, each requiring quick resolution. In middle management, problems take about twenty minutes to address but occur every ten minutes. At the senior management level, challenges are more complex, taking around sixty minutes to solve and arising every twenty minutes. At the executive and board level, problems are relentless, requiring action every five minutes and taking twenty-four hours to solve. To navigate this demanding landscape, organizations must cultivate aligned values, foster clear communication, ensure individual accountability, promote teamwork, and find profound meaning in their work.

How: Proverbs 29:2; Proverbs 11:14; Romans 12:3–8

NOVEMBER 6

Marriage is a sacrament within the church and stands as one of the most significant choices you will make in your life. It is essential to seek the guidance of the Holy Spirit when choosing your spouse. Avoid allowing emotions to rush you into a marriage decision. Your vows symbolize the seriousness of this commitment. You promise to be true to your spouse in good times and bad, in sickness and in health. You promise to love and honor your spouse all the days of your life. This commitment is made before God. Remember, the closer you both are to Jesus, the closer your relationship will become with each other.

How: Genesis 2:24; Ephesians 5:22–33; Matthew 19:6

_____

_____

_____

NOVEMBER 7

Be mindful of your nutrition plan. Take time each evening to plan your meals for the following day. Your body will tell you what it needs. This helps you avoid impulsive eating and the unnecessary intake of empty calories. Remember, many health issues arise from gut health. Focus on consuming lean proteins, vegetables, and fruits. Steer clear of alcohol, tobacco, sugar, processed foods, and deep-fried items. Additionally, be cautious not to overdo it on vitamins and supplements. Following this straightforward plan will help you maintain optimal performance.

How: Proverbs 23:20–21; Proverbs 25:27; Genesis 1:29–30

NOVEMBER 8

Hunting and fishing are essential skills that everyone should consider mastering. Even if these activities aren't your passion, understanding how to ethically harvest and process an animal can be crucial for survival. Moreover, it's vital to remain vigilant when handling firearms. Managing any weapon comes with significant responsibilities.

How: Genesis 27:3; Leviticus 17:13; Proverbs 12:27

NOVEMBER 9

An essential skill to cultivate in today's society is farming, which is one of the most physically demanding professions you can pursue. During my youth, I worked on a farm in Germany, and that experience equipped me for success in various aspects of life. It taught me valuable lessons in discipline, planning, humility, and both physical and mental resilience, while also instilling a deep reliance on God. I strongly encourage you to consider taking a summer job on a farm.

How: Ecclesiastes 11:4–6; James 5:7–8

NOVEMBER 10

The ideal time to purchase a snowblower is during the summer months. When it comes to buying a car, aim to do so at the end of the month or quarter for the best deals. It's wise to invest in older technology models when new versions are launched. To maintain financial health, avoid making impulsive purchases and always evaluate whether you truly need an item. Those who lack frugality often find themselves struggling financially in various aspects of life.

How: Proverbs 21:20; 1 Timothy 6:6–10

NOVEMBER 11

As you develop your skills and talents, you'll find that others will seek more of your time and energy. It's essential to learn how to say no. Be discerning about how you allocate your time and energy. It's important not to let others' disappointment affect you when you decline their requests. Remember, this isn't about being unkind; instead, it's a necessary form of self-care.

How: Matthew 5:37; 2 Timothy 1:7

_____

_____

NOVEMBER 12

Make it a daily priority to connect with your friends through conversation, not just text messages. A video call can uplift your spirits during tough times and amplify the joy in moments of happiness. Friendship is a precious gift from God, deserving of daily care and attention.

How: Proverbs 17:17; Proverbs 18:24; John 15:13

_____

_____

NOVEMBER 13

Autumn is my favorite season. Growing up in Michigan, I have a deep appreciation for the stunning colors that emerge as the leaves change. The air carries a refreshing crispness, and the harvests are gathered. As we look forward to the approaching Christmas season, it becomes a wonderful opportunity to express gratitude for all of God's blessings. Find ways to honor God during this special time of year.

How: Proverbs 3:9; 1 Corinthians 10:31; Psalm 29:2

NOVEMBER 14

Meditation is a valuable practice to cultivate. In today's fast-paced world, we are constantly surrounded by distractions that can scatter our thoughts. Before engaging in important tasks, I often take five to fifteen minutes to still my mind. This not only enhances my concentration but also allows me to consider new possibilities. Additionally, this practice is beneficial when facing stressful situations, as a calm mind wields great power.

How: Isaiah 26:3; Hebrews 12:2

NOVEMBER 15

Happiness is often temporary, reliant on external stimuli. The quest for happiness is even embedded in the United States Constitution. Yet, happiness can be short-lived; the things that once brought us fulfillment eventually lose their charm, memories fade, and the chase for happiness can become exhausting. Instead, aim for joy, as it comes from a wellspring that never runs dry.

How: Galatians 5:22–23; Psalm 16:11; 1 Peter 1:8–9

NOVEMBER 16

Sports teams transcend the games they participate in; they play a vital role in uniting communities, instilling hope in those who feel lost, and bringing families and nations together. It is essential to show respect for all sports teams and to appreciate their traditions and aspirations.

One of my cherished memories is of the 1980 USA Men's Olympic Hockey Team at Lake Placid. During a period when our nation faced significant challenges, we yearned for hope. The USA team consisted of relatively unknown young players, while the USSR team was recognized as the unrivaled best in the world. Against all odds, the USA team rose to the occasion, defeating the greatest team in history. This victory inspired our nation, instilling the belief that we could achieve anything.

How: Ecclesiastes 4:9–12; 2 Timothy 2:5

NOVEMBER 17

Consider a shocking news event from each of the following time-frames: last week, last month, last year, and last decade. As time passes, our ability to remember these significant occurrences diminishes, even when they captured the attention of every media outlet. The takeaway is straightforward: don't allow daily events to dictate your actions. Instead, stay true to your values and principles.

How: Proverbs 11:3; Romans 12:2

NOVEMBER 18

I once heard an intriguing story about the various types of individuals you might encounter in the military or any organization. Respectfully categorized, they are: Diligent, Clever, Stupid, and Lazy. Most individuals tend to exhibit a combination of two traits. Those who are Stupid and Lazy are typically best suited for routine tasks that require constant supervision. In contrast, those who are Clever and Diligent excel as staff officers or managers. People who are Clever and Lazy often thrive in top leadership positions, as they possess the intelligence and composure needed to make challenging decisions. The most concerning group, however, is the Diligent and Stupid, as they should not be entrusted with responsibilities; their actions lead to destruction and chaos.

How: Philippians 2:3; Proverbs 11:14

_____

_____

_____

NOVEMBER 19

Adopt the mindset of a general rather than that of an enlisted soldier. A general is adept at anticipating tactical and strategic maneuvers, often looking three to five steps ahead. They invest considerable time in observing and comprehending both their resources and their opponents. In contrast, enlisted soldiers focus primarily on executing the orders of their superiors. By thinking like a general, you can safeguard yourself against being taken by surprise in any situation.

How: Proverbs 21:5; Luke 14:28–33

NOVEMBER 20

I've experienced being cool, popular, and a bit eccentric. Ultimately, I find that embracing my weirdness is far more healthy and prosperous than anything else. Here are some principles I live by:

- Prioritize getting to bed early.
- Choose water instead of alcohol when out.
- Opt for fruits and vegetables as snacks.
- Embrace being the only one who hasn't seen the latest trend, and enjoy it.
- Stay out of the loop when it comes to celebrity gossip.
- Make time for reading books.
- Make quality time with your family a priority.
- Unplug from your phone for extended periods.
- Attend church every Sunday without fail.
- Practice kneeling in prayer.
- Save sexual intimacy for marriage.

How: Romans 12:2; 1 Peter 4:1–2; Isaiah 5:20

NOVEMBER 21

Avoid using TikTok or other social media platforms that entice you into consuming mindless content. Their artificial intelligence algorithms are engineered to keep you hooked. Likewise, it's wise to limit your time spent on video games for similar reasons. Excessive exposure to these distractions can have a profound impact on both your physical and mental well-being.

How: Romans 13:14; Ephesians 5:16

NOVEMBER 22

I have a kintsugi bowl on my desk in my office. Kintsugi is the traditional Japanese art of mending broken pottery using gold. Rather than concealing the damage, this technique accentuates the cracks and breaks, transforming them into a one-of-a-kind, beautiful piece. It serves as a metaphor for appreciating beauty in imperfections. Just like this bowl, we all carry scars and flaws in our lives. This bowl inspires me to celebrate the imperfections in ourselves and others as symbols of growth and beauty.

How: Corinthians 12:9; Romans 2:1

NOVEMBER 23

Embrace your fear zone. Regularly engage in activities that intimidate you, but steer clear of unnecessary risks to your safety. Focus on challenges like performing in front of an audience. Keep in mind that your initial attempts at anything new may not be perfect. True learning and growth occur when you confront your fears. If you don't confront these challenges, you may struggle to reach your full potential. Always remember that you are not alone in this journey.

How: Isaiah 41:10; Psalm 23:4; Psalm 27:1

_____

_____

_____

NOVEMBER 24

My mother had a close friend named Patricia, who was African American. During the Great Depression, my grandfather selflessly gave his only winter coat to a Native American man in need. Additionally, my father once sat next to Martin Luther King, Jr. on a flight, where they engaged in a meaningful discussion about race relations. It is crucial to reject racism and sexism in any form. Do not tolerate jokes or memes that undermine an individual's dignity. Surround yourself with people who share your values, and always approach situations like these with compassion and kindness. Use those moments as opportunities to educate and correct behavior that is harmful or disrespectful.

How: 1 Corinthians 12:13; 1 John 2:11; 1 Samuel 16:7

NOVEMBER 25

Remember to keep your marriage intentions in mind. Date with the intention to marry. It's advisable to steer clear of dating apps, as they often emphasize superficial qualities. Instead, seek connections in environments that align with your values, such as churches, special interest clubs, or charitable organizations. Establish clear boundaries and stay true to your values while getting to know your potential partner.

How: 1 Corinthians 13

NOVEMBER 26

I greatly admire Simon Sinek's insights and highly recommend his books. He once asked a thought-provoking question about brushing your teeth: "What does brushing your teeth for two minutes really accomplish?" The straightforward answer is, "Nothing, unless you do it twice a day, every day." This highlights the key lesson of prioritizing consistency over intensity. How often do we assess data and conclude that nothing is occurring, when, in reality, something meaningful might be unfolding? Don't be misled by the illusion of progress. Stay true to your values and remain steadfast on your path.

How: Philippians 1:6; Romans 5:3–5; Philippians 3:12–16

NOVEMBER 27

Exercise caution when sharing your photos online, even with friends. This is particularly important for images featuring yourself. A single photo can lead to unexpected repercussions. Your image and the things you say convey your values. A useful guideline is to consider whether this photo will portray you as humble in the eyes of God. Additionally, reflect on whether it could potentially cause jealousy or sadness in others.

How: Jeremiah 9:23–24; Proverbs 27:2

NOVEMBER 28

This is a delicate subject. I wholeheartedly believe that marriage is a sacred union ordained by God, where a man and a woman become one until death. Before embarking on this journey, there are numerous important discussions to have, including topics like children, intimacy, aspirations, faith, values, careers, and more. Financial matters also play an important role, as marriage is a legal contract. Considering a prenuptial agreement is a prudent decision as long as the focus remains on building a strong, Christ-centered marriage, rather than on anticipating its dissolution. While such an agreement might address financial matters, it should not undermine the spiritual and relational unity that marriage is intended to be. It's essential to remember that the closer you both are to Jesus, the stronger your bond will be in marriage.

How: Matthew 19:6; Ephesians 5; Genesis 2:24

NOVEMBER 29

What was the best meal you ever had? It's a difficult question to answer. If you can remember it clearly, chances are it was shared with family or friends. Throughout my life, I've enjoyed exquisite dishes at some of the finest restaurants around the world. However, when I reflect on this question, my thoughts don't drift to a remarkable culinary experience in Paris. Instead, I cherish memories of Thanksgiving dinner with my family, a delicious cheeseburger at Miller's Bar with my father-in-law, or a Big Mac from McDonald's with my mom after I finished mowing the lawn at age twelve. Ultimately, it's not just about the food; it's about the people you share it with.

How: Luke 14:12–14; Proverbs 15:17

NOVEMBER 30

Cultivating the habit of sending thoughtful, personalized messages can have a profound impact. A few heartfelt sentences are often enough, with handwritten notes being the most cherished—followed by digital messages. Keep a nice pen on hand and stock your desk with personal stationery and stamps, as this timeless practice brings joy to those who receive your words. Ultimately, while people may not recall your actions, they will always remember the feelings you inspired in them.

How: Ephesians 4:29; Hebrews 10:24–25; Romans 15:2

_____

_____

_____

DECEMBER 1

The wisdom I have gained over the past fifty years and shared in this book are intended to aid in your personal growth. This wisdom is profoundly personal, inspired by the Holy Spirit, and written with love for my cherished godchildren. I encourage you to continue seeking knowledge and wisdom. Immerse yourself in the works of great thinkers and writers such as Plato, Socrates, Shakespeare, Tolstoy, Faulkner, Kafka, the Saints, the Holy Bible, Walt Whitman, Frost, T.S. Eliot, John Milton, Homer, Longfellow, Rumi, Emerson, Robert Burns, Aristotle, Newton, Kant, Dante, Tesla, Einstein, Da Vinci, Euclid, Franklin, Marcus Aurelius, Descartes, Feynman, Mark Twain, Goethe, Dickens, Adam Smith, Abraham Lincoln, and Thomas Paine. These are just a few foundational thinkers to inspire your journey. Always ensure that any new ideas you encounter are tested and anchored in the teachings of the Holy Bible.

How: Proverbs 16:16; Proverbs 24:3–7; Ephesians 5:15–16

DECEMBER 2

When you choose to share your valuable advice, do so only when it's genuinely requested or in situations that could lead to harm if you don't speak up. Your talents and insights may create a strong urge to help others grow, but it's important to recognize that some individuals may not be prepared to receive your guidance. Unrequested advice often goes unheeded. Remember, your wisdom is a precious asset; treat it with the respect it deserves.

How: Proverbs 4:7; Proverbs 16:16; Proverbs 3:13–14

_____

_____

_____

DECEMBER 3

As I grow older, I find myself resonating more with Saint Peter. When Jesus called him to be an apostle, Peter humbly responded, "Depart from me, for I am a sinful man, O Lord!" Peter was humble. When Peter saw Jesus walking on water, he stepped out to join Him, yet he began to sink and cried out, "Lord, save me!" This demonstrates Peter's deep faith. When Jesus asked, "Who do you say I am?" Peter boldly proclaimed, "You are the Messiah, the Son of the living God." He had a personal relationship with Jesus. However, when confronted about being a disciple, Peter denied knowing Him, saying, "I don't know the man!" This shows his human frailty. Ultimately, after Peter had fallen and returned to his former occupation, Jesus reached out, asking, "Simon, son of John, do you love me?" Peter affirmed, "Yes, Lord; you know that I love you." In this, we see Peter's experience of love and forgiveness. This reflects life itself. Peter's intercession is a constant source of support in our lives, always ready to assist us through his prayers.

Prayer to Saint Peter:
O Holy Apostle, because you are the Rock upon which Almighty God has built His church; obtain for me I pray you, lively faith, firm hope, and burning love; complete detachment from myself, contempt of the world, patience in adversity, humility in prosperity, recollection in prayer, purity of heart, a right intention in all my works, diligence in fulfilling the duties of my state of life, constancy in my resolutions, resignation to the will of God and perseverance in the grace of God even unto death; that so, by means of your intercession and your glorious merits, I may be worthy to appear before the chief and eternal Shepherd of souls, Jesus Christ, Who with the Father and the Holy Spirit lives and reigns forever.

Amen.

How: Luke 5:11; Matthew 14:30–33; Matthew 16:13–20; Matthew 26:69–75; John 21:15

DECEMBER 4

"America is another name for opportunity," a famous quote attributed to Ralph Waldo Emerson, remains relevant across all stages of life and throughout the ages. Don't allow others to dictate what you can or cannot accomplish. Every day, countless Americans defy the odds to achieve remarkable feats. The distinction between those who succeed and those who do not is clear: it lies in consistency versus intensity. It involves refusing to let doubt take up residence in your mind, viewing challenges as opportunities for growth, and dedicating your efforts to the Lord Jesus Christ.

How: Proverbs 16:3; Ephesians 5:15–16; Galatians 6:10

DECEMBER 5

In environments filled with numerous rules, you often encounter a prevalence of uninspired and uncreative individuals. It's advisable to steer clear of such places, which can be found in every organization. Strict regulations foster a culture of compliance, while creativity and innovation flourish in an atmosphere of freedom. It's important to recognize the distinction between values and rules: values serve as guiding principles, while rules impose limitations.

How: Ephesians 2:10; Mark 7:7–13; Isaiah 10:1–2

DECEMBER 6

What kind of doer are you? How do you reach your goals? When faced with low energy, what strategies do you employ to motivate yourself? How do you maintain your focus? In challenging times, how do you obey God? These are questions worth pondering throughout your life. Understanding yourself goes beyond self-care; it is essential for achieving success. Many individuals develop a tendency to give up when they are unaware of how near they are to their goals. Additionally, many resort to distractions to avoid confronting their fears. A significant number of people struggle with focus, planning, assessment, and learning.

Consider running a marathon at least once in your life. This experience will provide you with profound insights to answer the questions posed above with clarity and conviction.

How: Romans 5:3–5; Romans 12:3

DECEMBER 7

Many years ago on this day, U.S. Navy sailors started their morning like any other in the idyllic setting of Hawaii. However, at 7:48 AM, everything changed as Japan launched a surprise attack on the United States Pacific Fleet stationed at Pearl Harbor. As time passes, we risk forgetting the horrors of that day. Lou Conter, the last survivor of the USS Arizona, passed away at the age of 102 in 2025. I encourage you to read about this pivotal moment, study its history, and learn from it. Most importantly, we must never forget and must honor the immense sacrifices made on that fateful day. Visiting the Pearl Harbor memorial at least once in your lifetime is an experience you should not miss.

How: John 15:13

DECEMBER 8

When I graduated from college, companies like Google, Facebook, Amazon, Nvidia, and Tesla did not yet exist. Every decade has a similar story to tell. Opportunities and innovations emerge every day. It's essential to position yourself with organizations that prioritize creating significant value for their customers. Moreover, the most successful companies structure their operations around the needs of their customers rather than solely focusing on their products. When organizations lose sight of this principle, they often fade away—a phenomenon that occurs more frequently than one might think.

How: Ephesians 5:16; Galatians 6:10; Matthew 7:12

DECEMBER 9

Christmas is a wonderful time to spread joy and hope to everyone. One of the best ways to embrace the season is by decorating your home with a Christmas tree and an Advent wreath. While this may seem simple, the hustle and bustle of daily life can easily distract us. It's important to remember the true meaning of Christmas. Sharing Christmas stories with children can be especially meaningful. During Advent, take the opportunity to do something uplifting for others. Personally, I've always cherished the experience of singing Christmas carols with groups at senior centers. Above all, let the joy of Christmas remain in your heart.

How: Isaiah 9:6; Matthew 2:10–12; Matthew 1:18–25

DECEMBER 10

When you establish a goal, keep it just between you and God. Refrain from sharing it with others or discussing your progress openly. Instead, let it reside quietly in your heart. Remember that all glory, honor, and praise belong to our Savior, Jesus Christ. Accomplishing your goal is not solely your achievement; it is the work of the Holy Spirit. Ultimately, it is God who created you and guides your journey.

How: 1 Corinthians 10:31; Psalm 115:1; Revelation 5:12–13

DECEMBER 11

People often respond thoughtlessly with harsh insults. The most effective response is often to remain silent. Such negativity stems from a hardened heart, usually fueled by jealousy of what you have. I won't deny that these words can sting, but if you can keep your composure and not let anger consume you, you've achieved a victory. Embrace forgiveness, just as Jesus forgave us. Recall His words on the cross: "Forgive them, Father, for they know not what they do." A heart filled with the Holy Spirit cannot hurl insults.

How: Luke 6:37; Ephesians 4:32; Matthew 18:21–22

DECEMBER 12

Certain individuals are unable to see and must depend on others for guidance. Others rely solely on their eyesight, which helps them to evade danger. Some perceive with both their eyes and their minds, enabling them to comprehend various situations effectively. There are those who engage their eyes, minds, and hearts, fostering deeper understanding and personal growth. However, only a select few perceive with their spirit, where true wisdom resides.

How: 1 Corinthians 2:14–16

_____

_____

_____

DECEMBER 13

Humor is a delightful gift that offers numerous benefits. Laughter triggers the release of hormones like dopamine, serotonin, endorphins, and oxytocin, all of which contribute to wellness, relaxation, pleasure, and feelings of euphoria. It serves as a powerful tool to help people transcend their instinctual fight-or-flight responses. In today's digital age, humor appears across social media in various formats, including memes. However, it's important to recognize that it can also be addictive. If not approached with caution, this form of humor may foster discord and intolerance. Always stay vigilant in public forums.

How: Proverbs 17:22; Psalm 126:2

_____

_____

_____

DECEMBER 14

Exercise caution when forming friendships with the opposite sex. While it's important to treat everyone with kindness and respect, true friendship goes beyond that; it necessitates nurturing and support. This commitment can take time away from other relationships and may lead to feelings of jealousy from family members. Additionally, you might inadvertently create a level of intimacy that is intended solely for your spouse.

How: 1 Timothy 5:1–2

DECEMBER 15

Bullying manifests in various ways and can occur at any stage of life. It is crucial to never accept this unacceptable behavior. Have the courage to confront bullies. Those who engage in bullying often struggle with low self-esteem, jealousy, anger management issues, or may have been victims of bullying themselves. There are numerous effective strategies for addressing a bully, but it is important to approach the situation with compassion. Stand up for those who are unable to defend themselves.

How: 1 Samuel 17

DECEMBER 16

Tragedies are an inevitable aspect of life. It's important to respect the diverse ways in which people cope with grief and stress, as each individual's experience is unique. As Cardinal Timothy Michael Dolan once articulated so beautifully, "Every time we encounter a tragedy, it presents an opportunity for renewal and transformation."

How: 2 Corinthians 1:3–4; Romans 8:28

DECEMBER 17

Avoid getting a tattoo for any reason! Your body is already perfect just as God created it. Remember, your body is a temple of the Holy Spirit. Don't try to rationalize the decision to get a tattoo. Beyond the potential health risks, it's a permanent choice that you might come to regret later on. As you grow older, a tattoo will magnify your physical decline. Ernest Hemingway once humorously suggested that relocating to Boca Raton to start a tattoo removal clinic would be one of the wisest investments one could make.

How: Leviticus 19:28; Corinthians 6:19

DECEMBER 18

In any competitive setting, whether in sports, academics, or other fields, aim to position yourself among the top competitors. Surprisingly, competing at this elite level often requires less physical and mental effort. This is primarily because everyone is focused on striving for victory. In contrast, the most challenging aspect of competition occurs in the "cutoff zone," where competitors are not only striving for their own success but also working to surpass each other. This creates a tug-of-war dynamic that can be exhausting and depleting.

How: 1 Corinthians 9:24–27; Philippians 2:3–4; Philippians 3:13–14

DECEMBER 19

Pray sincerely for those who do not have Christ in their hearts. Their lives are often filled with unimaginable struggles and turmoil. While believers in Christ also face their own challenges, our sufferings serve a purpose in our journey toward sanctification. During Mass, before the Holy Eucharist is shared, the priest proclaims, "Peace I leave with you, my peace I give to you." Let us pray that those who do not believe will experience this perfect peace.

How: Romans 10:9–10; Matthew 7:16–20; John 14:27

DECEMBER 20

Your purpose here is not to seek entertainment or to be entertained; these are worldly pursuits. Instead, focus on Jesus as your guiding North Star. This entails embracing your cross daily and following Him. Avoid the temptation of finding comfort in worldly distractions. Rather, find your strength in resting in Jesus Christ during your moments of weakness.

How: Matthew 11:28–30; Matthew 16:24

DECEMBER 21

Always avoid doing work for free. Instead, consider offering a significant discount or exchanging your services for something like a meal. This principle holds true whether you're dealing with family, professional situations, or volunteer opportunities. Providing work without compensation sends the message that your services lack value, which is simply not the case. This lesson was imparted to me by my mentor early in my career. When you consistently give away your work for free, it can lead you to undervalue yourself. Additionally, those who accept free services are less likely to respect your expertise and effort.

How: Ephesians 4:28; Colossians 3:23–24

_____

_____

_____

DECEMBER 22

Taking just sixty seconds can help you avoid a regrettable mistake. Pause, pray, breathe, and then take action. This simple process has proven invaluable in emergency situations where time is of the essence. In moments of urgency, the urge to respond immediately can be overwhelming. Yet, you can always spare a minute to collect your thoughts before proceeding. The power of that minute is significant. On the other hand, sixty seconds spent in anger, lust, greed, or any sin can lead to disastrous consequences. Remember, take a moment: Pause, pray, breathe, then act.

How: Philippians 4:6–7; Psalm 46:1; Deuteronomy 31:6

DECEMBER 23

I dedicate this book to Saint Carlo Acutis. I encourage you to explore his remarkable contributions during his brief time on Earth. He exemplified a profound love for God, embodying devotion in heart, mind, strength, and spirit. Here are a few of his inspiring insights:

"Sadness is looking at ourselves, happiness is looking toward God."

"Everyone is born original, but most end up dying as photocopies."

"We are all likely to fall short because as soon as someone says something we don't like, we instantly grow angry."

"Not me, but God."

How: 1 Corinthians 1:2; Romans 1:7; Revelation 5:8

DECEMBER 24

Cherish your family's Christmas traditions while also embracing the opportunity to create new ones. Always attend Christmas Eve Mass with your loved ones. Most importantly, carry the spirit of Christmas joy in your heart throughout the entire year.

How: Luke 2:11; Matthew 1:21; Isaiah 9:6

_____

_____

_____

DECEMBER 25

Welcome to the most wonderful morning of the year! Whether you're sleeping in or waking up early, consider yourself fortunate to be surrounded by loved ones. If you pause and listen closely, you'll notice a unique calmness in the air. The usual hustle and bustle gives way to gentle whispers of love from God. Savor every moment of this day, and have a truly Merry Christmas!

How: Luke 2:11; Matthew 1:21; Isaiah 9:6

_____

_____

_____

DECEMBER 26

When you enter college, you may feel significant pressure to join a fraternity or sorority. I personally chose to join a fraternity and forged lifelong friendships, for which I am thankful. However, it's important to recognize that these organizations often foster environments conducive to alcohol abuse. This can adversely affect your academic and athletic performance. Therefore, exercise caution and be discerning about the organizations you choose to associate with in college. Successful individuals tend to avoid activities that could jeopardize their physical and mental well-being.

How: Ephesians 5:18; Romans 13:13; Proverbs 23:20–21

DECEMBER 27

I have encountered individuals who fail to respond to my messages regarding meeting requests. This behavior is commonly referred to as "ghosting," and it comes across as unprofessional. In these situations, it's easy to feel anger. However, it's important to recognize that your frustration may be rooted in your own ego; we often tend to view ourselves as the most important person in any situation.

There can be numerous reasons for someone to ghost you, many of which may have nothing to do with you personally. Rather than using this as an opportunity to express discontent, consider forgiving them and wishing them well. Furthermore, refrain from sharing your insights or assistance, as they may not value your input.

Lastly, always strive to respond to others in a professional manner. Even if you need to decline a request, do so with kindness and empathy.

How: Colossians 3:23; 2 Timothy 2:15

DECEMBER 28

My beloved mother dedicated forty years of her life to teaching reading in an underserved school district in Michigan. She played a pivotal role in helping a generation learn to read, and the positive effects of her work are immeasurable. Despite holding multiple academic degrees and earning a commendable salary, she chose to drive a modest gray Buick Century rather than a Cadillac. When I inquired about her decision, she explained, "The students I serve come from very disadvantaged backgrounds, often with only one parent at home. I wouldn't want to draw attention to myself." Her commitment is a beautiful example of honoring God over oneself.

How: Psalm 29:2; Psalm 96:9; Proverbs 3:9

_____

_____

_____

DECEMBER 29

Live your life in accordance with God's will rather than the distractions of the world. When worldly matters demand your attention and you have a sacred obligation to attend Mass, prioritize what is Holy. Hold Psalm 1:1–2 close to your heart!

"Blessed is the man who walks not in the counsel of the wicked, nor stands in the way of sinners, nor sits in the seat of scoffers; but his delight is in the law of the Lord, and on His law he meditates day and night."

How: Psalm 1:1–2; John 14:15; 1 John 5:3

_____

_____

_____

DECEMBER 30

You may be familiar with the seven deadly sins, but they hold no power against the seven holy virtues. Temptation is an inevitable part of life. When you face it, concentrate on the corresponding virtue. Seek guidance and protection through prayer to our Lord Jesus Christ, who is always with you.

Sin:	Holy Virtue:
Greed	Charity
Lust	Chasity
Sloth	Diligence
Pride	Humility
Envy	Kindness
Wrath	Patience
Gluttony	Temperance

How: Galatians 5:16; Romans 6:6; 1 Corinthians 10:13

_____

_____

_____

DECEMBER 31

To my cherished godchildren, wherever you may be today and whatever you may be doing, I want you to know that I am praying for you wholeheartedly to the Lord Jesus Christ. I extend this sentiment to anyone reading this book. Let us honor God today by performing a random act of kindness for someone in need.

How: Galatians 6:10; Ephesians 4:32

RIVERSHORE BOOKS

www.rivershorebooks.com
info@rivershorebooks.com